The ADHD Guide to Career Success: Harness Your Strengths, Manage Your Challenges

Just as the classroom poses the greatest challenges for children and teens with ADHD, the workplace is the arena in which adult ADHD poses the greatest threat. And while adults with ADHD are likely to face professional challenges, it is possible to cultivate a work environment that enables them to thrive and use the strengths of this unique condition to their advantage. Featuring a large open format with summaries at the beginning of each chapter and designed with the ADHD reader in mind, this newly revised and updated edition offers an easy-to-follow progression of useful information interwoven with practical strategies for career success.

Kathleen Nadeau, PhD, is a clinical psychologist and director of the Chesapeake ADHD Center in Silver Spring, Maryland, where she continues to practice. She has been a leader in the field for the past 20 years, publishing more than a dozen books on topics related to ADHD. In 1999, she received the CHADD Hall of Fame Award for her groundbreaking work on women and girls with ADHD. Dr. Nadeau is a frequent lecturer both nationally and internationally, focusing on her solution-focused, integrative approach to treating ADHD. She has focused for many years on issues relating to careers and employment for those with ADHD and is currently developing the ADHD Career Center to provide strengths-based, ADHD–aware career exploration and career coaching to college students and adults.

The ADHD Guide to Career Success

Harness Your Strengths, Manage Your Challenges

Kathleen Nadeau

NEW YORK AND LONDON

First published 2016
by Routledge
711 Third Avenue, New York, NY 10017

and by Routledge
27 Church Road, Hove, East Sussex BN3 2FA

Routledge is an imprint of the Taylor & Francis Group, an informa business

Library of Congress Cataloging-in-Publication Data
A catalog record for this book has been requested

ISBN: 978-1-138-84366-0 (pbk)
ISBN: 978-1-315-72333-4 (ebk)

Typeset in Times New Roman
by Apex CoVantage, LLC

Contents

Don't usually read books? Never fear—this book is written in an ADHD-friendly, easy-to-read style. This chapter introduces you to the main ideas of the book: that you need to identify and harness your strengths and learn to manage your ADHD challenges, identifying the best job setting for your unique needs. I'll teach you how to do this in the chapters that follow.

1

Harness Your Strengths, Manage Your Challenges: An Overview

If you are starting to read this book, chances are you are an adult with attention deficit hyperactivity disorder (ADHD) or the parent of a young adult with ADHD who is trying to learn as much as possible about how to choose or change to a career path in which you (or your loved one) can succeed. The first thing to understand is that there are huge differences among individuals with ADHD—so there is no one-size-fits-all answer to finding a successful career path. You are more than your ADHD—you are a complex individual with interests, abilities, education, experience, and temperament that have to be taken into account as well to find a career path that allows you to function at your best.

First, I'd Like to Introduce You to How to Use This Book

If you're like many adults with ADHD, you may have difficulty staying focused on a book long enough to finish it. Don't worry. This book is designed to be ADHD friendly. Don't feel obliged to read straight through it from beginning to end. The best approach is to thumb through the book (chapter topics listed in the margins make it easier to find what you're looking for). Then read the brief description located at the beginning of a chapter that catches your eye. By reading the summary, you can quickly decide whether to continue or to move on to a topic more relevant to you and your circumstances.

The Format

Other ADHD–friendly features of this book are that information is presented in "digestible bites" suitable for people who have difficulty with extended concentration. Even people without concentration problems will appreciate the book's convenient format.

- A descriptive synopsis at the beginning of each chapter
- A clear writing style
- Personal stories that can illustrate and help you relate to topics covered in the book
- Catchphrases designed to help you recall key ideas
- Chapter topics printed in the right-hand margins of each page, allowing you to thumb through the book to easily find what you're looking for
- Clear labels for the sections and subsections of each chapter that together create a chapter outline, emphasizing key points
- Open layout with more white space to reduce eyestrain
- Visual stimulation through good graphic design

"ADHD Friendly"
=
"User Friendly"

Catchphrases (Aphorisms)

Benjamin Franklin was a master of aphorisms and used many in *Poor Richard's Almanack*:[1]

Most of us are familiar with some of his sayings, such as:

A stitch in time saves nine.

Never put off until tomorrow what you can do today.

Early to bed and early to rise makes a man healthy, wealthy, and wise.

There are some ADHD experts who even suggest that Benjamin Franklin was an adult with ADHD who developed effective tools for memory and organization as ways to compensate for his ADHD symptoms![2] As you can see, many of his best-known sayings relate directly to difficulties experienced by most adults with ADHD.

Following Ben Franklin's example, you will find ADHD–friendly advice throughout this book presented in brief, easy-to-remember fashion, such as:

A short list is better than a long memory!

or

Do it now or write it down!

These phrases are ADHD–friendly memory tools to help you remember the essence of what I explore at greater length.

As children with ADHD leave their school years behind, work becomes the arena of challenge and opportunity. This book is written in an effort to provide much-needed assistance to young adults as they make career choices and to mid-career adults who may find themselves struggling in jobs or careers that prove to be a poor match for them. I'll also offer lots of tips for people who want to perform better at work. Sometimes the problem is not a poor job match but rather the need to develop habits and systems to be more productive and effective. The information you'll find in this book is derived from my experience over the course of several decades in working with adults with ADHD who have job-related concerns.

Many of the things we do at work require the skills taught during our school years. At work, most of us must read, write, make calculations, organize and carry out projects, meet deadlines, learn new information, and pay attention during meetings and lectures. The difference is that there are many choices once school years are over. These choices make it easier to find work that does not require you to function primarily in areas of weakness. One goal of this book is to help you to understand your ideal work environment and then help you to find or create a work environment that meets your needs. Of course, no work environment is a perfect match, but the better you understand your needs, the better you can accurately assess how well you will function in jobs you are considering.

The ideal job for you is not only determined by your challenges. Even more important are your gifts, talents, and interests that will make certain careers much more satisfying and successful than others. In the chapters to come, I will help you learn to advocate for your needs at work, teach you techniques to better manage your ADHD symptoms at work, and help you understand the workplace environment in which you will function best. What you learn from this book will increase your odds of making ADHD–smart workplace choices.

Over the years, adults with ADHD have taught me a great deal that I will pass along to you. The process of understanding their patterns, struggles, and successes has been one of mutual discovery for my clients and me. Many have developed ingenious and effective means of coping with their challenges. Their self-observations, their perspective on career success and failure, and the techniques they have developed to cope with frustrating ADHD symptoms have been incorporated in this book. While this book was written primarily for adults with ADHD, it can also be useful for relatives, employers, coworkers, and career counselors as well.

Harnessing Your Strengths—Some ADHD Traits Can Lead to Career Success

Most of what you will read about ADHD views it as a "disability" or "condition" that requires "treatment." In contrast to this disability model, I have come to think of ADHD as a type of brain—one that struggles with certain types of tasks but also one that brings with it characteristics that can be tremendously positive in the right context. The very traits that may have caused you difficulty during your school years may become the traits that can lead to your career success. Hyperactivity can translate into the drive and high energy so typical of successful entrepreneurs. Risk taking that can lead to broken bones in childhood can morph into a willingness to take risks that is necessary for the entrepreneur or creative adult. Curiosity that may have resulted in distractibility during school years can lead an ADHD adult to see unlikely connections and new discoveries.

How Common Is ADHD?

The behaviors related to ADHD are among the most common reasons children are referred for psychological treatment. Statistics vary, but a CDC report in 2011[3] states that approximately 11% of the school-age population had been diagnosed with ADHD. Other reports suggest that approximately 60% of children with ADHD continue to have significant symptoms of ADHD in adulthood. In 2006,[4] a study found that between 4 and 5% of adults have ADHD. Certainly, a much greater percentage of adults struggle significantly with some aspects of ADHD. While there are those who believe the majority of children with ADHD outgrow their symptoms, ADHD is a lifelong condition to some extenxt for the majority of those who are affected.

ADHD is a genuine neurobiological disorder, one that, if untreated, can cause enormous difficulty and suffering in the lives of those who have it. ADHD is a condition that deserves careful diagnosis by a trained professional, a diagnosis that should only be made if symptoms have a long-term, significant effect on the functioning of an individual. That said, most of what you'll read about ADHD in the media only focuses on the challenges of ADHD, giving the public a very negative view of the condition. Those of us who work in the field deplore media coverage that trivializes, misrepresents, or sensationalizes ADHD.

The Struggle to Receive Acceptance and Understanding

In the work-obsessed American culture, the recent publicity about ADHD seems to have sparked a debate that places two strongly held attitudes at odds with one another.

The "Just Do It!" School of Thought

Because hard work and self-discipline are values so engrained in our American culture, it is easy for some to condemn those with ADHD as lazy, morally inferior, or excuse seeking. We in this land of the free and home of the brave like to believe individuals have the capacity to exert full control over their actions and reactions. This approach to life might be described as the "Just do it!" school of thought. It's very tempting to believe life can be that simple, that if we just try hard enough, we can conquer anything. The facts are, however, that no one can be good at everything, no matter how hard he or she tries. A smarter approach is to discover what you're best at and to find or create supports to help you perform better in areas of challenge.

Scientific Understanding of Behavior

Equally strong as the "just do it" philosophy is our belief in science and technology. As we lead the world in medical research, we Americans take great pride in our increasing understanding of neuroscience. With our more sophisticated understanding of brain processes, we are moving away from a simplistic, moralistic approach to behavior and toward an enlightened, scientific-treatment-oriented approach.

If we look at ADHD in the light of our growing understanding of the neurochemistry and neurophysiology underlying the condition, it becomes difficult for us to cling to the "just do it" school of thought. Neuroscience is gradually unveiling the complexities of the brain, demonstrating that who we are is profoundly influenced, even controlled, by brain structure and brain chemistry.

An ADHD diagnosis is an explanation, NOT an excuse.

The risk in understanding ADHD as a neurological disorder is to overemphasize that ADHD symptoms are not the fault of the individual and to underemphasize the individual's responsibility and capacity to manage his or her disorder. The Americans with Disabilities Act (5)[5] doesn't relieve adults with ADHD of responsibility for taking charge of their disability; it only attempts to describe a limited but important role employers can play in supporting them in the workplace (for more information about the Americans with Disabilities Act, see Chapter 12).

A diagnosis of ADHD doesn't divest people of responsibility for the difficulties they experience; it only provides a framework for understanding and learning to manage this challenging disability.

Managing Your Challenges—Taking Charge of ADHD

The healthiest attitude toward attention deficit disorder can be summed up in this phrase:

Take charge of your ADHD so it doesn't take charge of you!

How can you take charge? Here are some suggestions:

1. Educate yourself as much as possible about ADHD.
2. Make an accurate ADHD self-assessment.
3. Seek appropriate help for your ADHD.
4. Learn techniques to minimize your ADHD symptoms.
5. Recognize and use your positive traits.
6. Make the most informed and appropriate career choice or change.
7. Learn ways to make your job more ADHD friendly.
8. Learn how to appropriately advocate for yourself at work.

This book is designed to help you make a good career choice and learn how to take charge of your ADHD at work so you can focus all your energies on building a successful and satisfying career.

Notes

1 Franklin, B. (1759). *Poor Richard's Almanack.*
2 Hartmann, T. (1993). *Attention Deficit Disorder: A Different Perception.* Penn Valley, CA: Underwood-Miller.
3 http://www.cdc.gov/ncbddd/adhd/data.html
4 Kessler RC, Adler L, Barkley R, Biederman J, Conners CK, et al. (2006). The prevalence and correlates of adult ADHD in the United States: results from the National Comorbidity Survey Replication. *Am J Psychiatry*. Apr; 163(4):716–23.
5 Americans With Disabilities Act, U.S. Code, vol. 42, sees. 12101 et seq (1990).

This chapter emphasizes that when you have ADHD, it's important that your career assessment focus more on your strengths than on your challenges, taking into account your abilities, not just "disabilities" related to ADHD. The more a career focuses on your interests and strengths and suits your personal style, the less your ADHD will impact workplace performance.

2

Strengths-Focused ADHD Career Assessments

Not sure what you want to be when you grow up? Whether you are in high school, in college wondering what your major should be, or recently graduated and confused about how to chart your career course, a strengths-focused ADHD career assessment can help you identify a career path that is a good match for you. You will need an assessment that identifies strengths, interests, areas of weakness, and personality type, as well as the particular ADHD challenges you experience.

How Do I Find Someone to Evaluate ADHD Workplace Issues?

It can be very difficult to find an ADHD specialist who is well versed in career issues and equally difficult to find a career counselor knowledgeable about ADHD. You may need to work simultaneously with both an ADHD specialist and a career counselor in order to really address the whole range of pertinent issues. In selecting an ADHD specialist, ask the following questions:

1. How much of your practice consists of working with *adults* who have ADHD?
2. Have you worked extensively on career issues with ADHD adults?
3. Do you have experience with the Myers-Briggs Type Indicator and its use on career issues?
4. Do you use the Strong Interest Inventory[1] as part of your career assessment for adults with ADHD?
5. Are you familiar with the Highlands Ability Battery[2] that is designed to measure a wide range of abilities that can help identify a good career match?
6. Would you feel comfortable working in collaboration with a career counselor to help me address my career concerns?

What Needs to Be Considered in a Career Assessment?

All of you, not just your ADHD, needs to be considered in your career assessment. An assessment that only focuses on ADHD symptoms won't be very useful if you are poorly matched with your career. Although a good career match is important for everyone, it is *essential* for adults with ADHD. Why? It is almost *impossible* for adults with ADHD to succeed in careers that don't interest them! A good match should take advantage of your strengths, minimize your areas of weakness, and be interesting enough to grab your attention.

If you desire a full career evaluation, the process you go through should include all of the assessment techniques discussed previously, plus an evaluation of interests and abilities.

Interests

There are a number of "interest tests" you can take. They are often offered at university counseling centers and by career counselors. Many psychologists also have been trained in interpreting interest testing. Three of the most common interest tests are the Self-Directed Search,[3] the Strong Interest Inventory,[4] and the Vocational Preference Inventory.[5] In general, these tests compare your stated interests with the interests of people who have been successful in various career fields. They provide you with a list of careers that most closely match your stated interests.

In the classic career book *What Color Is Your Parachute?*[6] Richard Bolles describes less formal ways of analyzing interest patterns. One of these exercises is to imagine a party at which there are six "types" of people (based on the interest tests mentioned). He then asks you to imagine yourself at this party and to decide which groups of people you would feel most drawn to, in order from "most" to "least." The initials used to identify the first three groups on your preference list make up your "Holland code"[7] or career type. Your choices of groups at this imaginary party are:

"Realistic" types—People who are oriented toward engineering, building, and athletics. They prefer to work with tools, plants, and machines, and often prefer to be outdoors.

"Investigative" types—People who like to analyze, learn, investigate, and problem solve. Many of these "investigators" are scientists.

"Artistic" types—People who are intuitive, creative, imaginative, and unstructured.

"Social" types—People who enjoy working with people and are good with words. They are often teachers, counselors, ministers, or other types of helpers.

"Enterprising" types—These people like to influence, persuade, manage, or lead others in business enterprises.

"Conventional" types—People who like to work with data, facts, and details and are comfortable carrying out instructions.

By imagining what group you would feel most drawn to and most comfortable with at this imaginary party, you are indirectly assessing your own cluster of interests and tendencies.

There is no right way to assess interests. Taking a test is not necessarily more accurate than the "imaginary party" exercise described by Bolles. Take a look at checklists in a number of books on choosing careers. No matter how you decide to assess your interests, do it in an active fashion, and take the idea of analyzing your interests seriously. A high degree of career interest is more important for an adult with ADHD than for most others. Why? Because a high interest level is one of the most powerful antidotes to distractibility and difficulty sustaining your attention! When you're very interested in an activity, you can lock in your focus and often maintain concentration for long periods of time. We call this pattern "hyperfocus." The ability to hyperfocus is a great asset for those with the good fortunate to be well matched with their careers.

Skills and Abilities

When you are concerned about ADHD, it is easy to dwell too much on the things you don't do well and forget to focus on your skills and abilities.

Do a personal skills assessment. Make a list of things you do well (and *like* to do). Don't leave anything out just because it doesn't seem applicable to a career. Make as complete a list as you can. It may be useful to talk to a close friend or family member, who may remind you of things you are overlooking. Your list might include things like:

Enjoy talking with people

Good at making people laugh

Good with my hands

Good cook

Love to read

Good at writing

Good at taking care of young children

Good driver

Good at crossword puzzles

Good at playing Trivial Pursuit

Good athlete

In addition to a self-assessment, it can be very useful to take an ability test. One of the best known is offered by the Johnson-O'Connor Research Foundation.[8] Another ability test is the Highlands Ability Battery.[9] Both of these test batteries measure your ability across a wide range of activities. Their reports cluster your abilities and match these clusters with careers that call for such talents.

Personal Circumstances

Even after you have gathered all the information regarding interests and abilities, you still have important choices to make. For example, an assessment that concludes that you are ideally suited to become an architect isn't helpful if the time and resources aren't available to you to train for this career! A good assessment helps you choose the best fit for you within realistic options, considering personal factors such as:

Age

Health

Financial resources

Time availability—considering other commitments, such as family commitments

Feasibility/desirability of additional education or training

The ideal career match must be realistic, taking into account all your personal circumstances. At the same time, don't be afraid to dream. I have worked with many people who made bold decisions to change career direction in midlife, made tremendous efforts to achieve their goals, and felt it was the best decision they ever made.

Summary

To summarize, an ADHD career assessment should help you consider carefully all the following issues:

1. How you are specifically affected at work by ADHD
2. Whether your work performance is impacted by learning disabilities
3. What ADHD coping strategies would be best for you
4. What on-the-job accommodations would be appropriate
5. What your work history reveals about jobs that are ADHD-friendly for you
6. Your personality type and how it impacts a career choice
7. Which career choices are compatible with your interests
8. Your unique mosaic of abilities and weaknesses
9. The impact of your personal circumstances on career options

The summary of your ADHD career assessment should list which career options are a good match for you—that is, those that call primarily on your greatest strengths while minimizing performance demands in your areas of weakness.

The process of making a good career choice or career change is complex. Working with your ADHD career counselor following the assessment phase will be time well spent. Resist a typical ADHD tendency to leap to a decision and carefully consider, with your counselor, all the factors listed above. Finding the ideal career match is well worth the work involved. A good career match (and job match within that career) can make all the difference in reaching a successful and satisfying work life.

What If What I Need Is a Different Job, Not a Different Career?

There's a big difference between a **job** and a **career.** Often people confuse the two. You could be in the right career but in the wrong job. What's the difference? A career is a very broad collection of jobs that all relate to the same general field. For example, you might choose a career in the computer field. There are many different jobs within this field, however. You could be a programmer, a technician, a salesperson, an administrator, a software developer, or a teacher or trainer. The same is true for almost every career field. Your task is to find a career field that interests you and then to find a particular type of job within that field that is a good match for your strengths and interests.

If you are still in school and are in the process of choosing a career path, you need to think both about a *career* and about finding a particular *job* within that career. If you are already out in the working world, your first question will probably be, "How can I function better in my current job?" Later, if you and your ADHD career counselor conclude that you are very poorly matched with your current job/career, you may want to consider a job change or even a career change.

Notes

1 Strong Interest Inventory, published by CPP, Inc., Sunnyvale, CA, www.cpp.com.
2 Highlands Ability Battery, published by the Highlands Company, www.highlandsco.com.
3 Self-Directed Search, published by PAR, found at www.self-directed-search.com.
4 Strong Interest Inventory, published by CPP, Inc., Sunnyvale, CA, www.cpp.com.
5 Vocational Preference Inventory (VPI), published by PAR, found at career.iresearch-net.com/career_?vocational-preference-inventory-vpi/.
6 Bolles, Richard. (2015). *What Color is Your Parachute? 2015: A Practical Manual for Job Hunters and Career-Changers.* Berkley, CA: Ten Speed Press.
7 Holland Codes or the Holland Occupational Themes (RIASEC) refers to a theory of careers and vocational choices (based upon personality types) that was initially developed by psychologist John L. Holland (1919–2008).
8 Johnson O'Connor Research Foundation is a nonprofit scientific research and educational organization that offers career aptitude testing and conducts research on human abilities in relationship to career functioning. 1120 Connecticut Ave. N.W. # 1060, Washington, DC, 20036.
9 Highlands Ability Battery is an online computerized ability testing tool that provides individuals with career paths best suited to their patterns of natural ability. www.highlandsco.com.

In this chapter, you will be guided through a self-assessment of potential problem areas on the job. It will be useful to complete the ADHD Workplace Questionnaire in the Appendix before reading this chapter.

3

Guided Self-Assessments to Address On-the-Job Challenges

Are you in a crisis at work? Afraid you might lose your job? Many adults seek assessment to answer questions that are immediate, urgent, and practical: How can I improve performance in my current job so I don't lose it? This type of workplace assessment should focus on:

- How your ADHD specifically affects your job performance
- Whether coexisting learning disabilities are impacting your performance
- What coping strategies can help you take charge of ADHD challenges
- What accommodations your employer can provide
- How your personality type affects a good job match
- What aspects of prior jobs have or have not worked well for you

Let's consider each of these areas of concern separately.

Current Job Functioning

I have developed the *Adult ADHD Workplace Questionnaire* (found in the Appendix) to help you pinpoint exactly how ADHD impacts your functioning in your particular job. This questionnaire was developed to help you and your career specialist evaluate the on-the-job impact of your ADHD. It is divided into categories in order to help you organize this self-assessment. It also can be very useful to obtain the feedback of a trusted friend or close colleague in making this self-assessment.

Coexisting Learning Problems

On the Workplace Questionnaire, there is a section titled "Other Cognitive Problems." If you answered "yes" to a number of these questions, you may be struggling with learning differences that may impact your functioning at work. The tests appropriate for evaluating learning disorders in adults will not be listed here because they need to be selected by a learning disorders (LD) specialist. The type of testing that would be appropriate depends on the types of learning problems that are suspected.

The combination of LD with ADHD is very common, although many adults were never evaluated for learning problems when they were children. Such learning problems, even in their mildest form, can cause significant problems on the job.

You might ask, "Why bother about learning disorders now? I'm already finished with school." The answer is that even when we are through with school, we are *never* through with the tasks taught in school—reading, writing, and making calculations. And in today's workforce, we are never through with learning. To remain competitive and employable, we are expected to learn new things. Many areas of difficulty can be improved through remedial tutoring, even in adulthood.

Testing for learning disorders can help your ADHD career professional guide you to a better job match or career choice.

Reasonable Accommodations

To determine, with your counselor, which types of accommodations would be most helpful and appropriate for you, refer to Chapter 13, which lists a range of possible accommodations for ADHD in the workplace. Be sure to read Chapter 12 on the Americans with Disabilities Act to better understand the responsibilities of your employer. Your employer is not expected to know what accommodations you may need if you have an ADHD diagnosis and is only required to provide accommodations that are deemed "reasonable" for your particular employer to provide.

Personality Type at Work

Your personality type is so important to making good career and workplace recommendations that Chapter 5 has been devoted to discussing personality types, as measured by the Myers-Briggs Type Indicator (MBTI),[1] and how different personality types require different kinds of ADHD coping strategies and have different ideal career matches. The MBTI is brief, usually inexpensive, and can provide extremely valuable information to help you determine your best workplace strategies.

Employment History

In order to evaluate your employment history from an ADHD perspective, you should conduct an informal job analysis with the help of your career consultant, considering each position you have held, including your current position. You will find a list of questions in what follows to help you structure this job analysis.

ADHD Job Analysis

1. What were the "pluses" in this job?

2. What were the "minuses"?

(List anything you can think of in making each of these lists. Your list might include things such as pay, opportunity for advancement, my supervisor, my coworkers, commuting time, types of assigned tasks, variety, challenge, interest, general work-place environment, etc.)

3. What were my primary challenges on this job?

   (a) Were these problems ADHD related?

   (b) Were these problems ones I could reduce or eliminate by taking charge of my ADHD, learning habits, and coping skills?

   (c) Did these problems call for accommodations from my employer?

   (d) Were these problems ones over which I had no influence or control?

4. How ADHD friendly was my job in terms of:

   My boss

   My work assignments

   The structure of the job

   The level of distractions

   The repetitive nature of the work

   The interest level

   The general atmosphere

   The level of paperwork requirements

   The level of administrative support

Cognitive Functioning

It can be very helpful to understand your relative cognitive strengths and weaknesses. A neuropsychological evaluation can be very valuable to help you and your career counselor understand your verbal skills, analytical skills, working memory skills, processing speed, cognitive flexibility, and visual-spatial skills, among others. Such an assessment can also help you understand your organizational and planning skills in comparison to others of your general age and ability. The more you understand about yourself and your abilities, the better able you will be to choose a career path that is a good match for you.

Can Your Current Job *Become* the Right Job?

If you are like some individuals with ADHD, your first instinct may be to say, "Forget about this job! I'm sick of it!" But don't be so quick! It's a tempting fantasy to believe that a fresh start somewhere else will be better. But, if you think back, you have probably had a number of fresh starts where problems began to develop once again.

Even if you are fairly sure you want to leave your current position, your ADHD-smart move may be to stay for the time being. Why?

- You can practice building new success habits and developing success traits on this job so you will be in a better position to get and keep your next job.
- An improvement in performance and attitude will win you a much more positive recommendation when seeking another job.

Conducting an ADHD Job Analysis

Your ADHD job analysis is your blueprint for exploring what needs to change in order to function well in your current job. Try to divide changes into two groups: internal and external.

External changes could also be thought of as "environmental" changes—changes in your physical work environment, changes in the tasks that are assigned to you, changes in how you are mentored or supervised, and changes in the degree of collaboration at work. External changes could include:

1. Change of supervisor
2. Using assistive technologies (computers, software, e-mail, electronic beepers, recorders, daily agendas, etc.)
3. More structure
4. More autonomy
5. Less distracting work environment
6. More teamwork
7. More administrative support
8. More interesting, challenging assignments
9. Less stressful work environment (define)

Think of more on your own. This list is just a start. Chapter 13 on accommodations and Chapter 16 on assistive technology may be helpful to you in devising this list.

Internal Changes—Internal changes are ways you change yourself. You need to ask, What kinds of changes do I need to make within myself? Internal changes might include:

1. Interacting differently with your supervisor
2. Developing ways to compensate for ADHD challenges
3. Developing a more positive attitude and more constructive habits. Look at Chapter 13 on "ADHD Success Strategies."
4. Improving organizational and time management skills

Some of these changes can be accomplished on your own, but you may find it helpful to work with an ADHD job coach or specialist.

Putting It All Together

After you have gone through all these steps with your ADHD career counselor, including a careful analysis of how ADHD affects your functioning on your current job, considering possible learning disorders, looking at your personality type, the best accommodations and coping strategies, and making a careful analysis of prior jobs, your counselor should be ready to write a highly detailed and specific report, carefully outlining what assistance you may need from a tutor or job coach, what coping strategies you should develop, and what reasonable accommodations you should need from your employer.

Your ADHD career counselor should write an all-inclusive report for you, as well as a letter to your employer outlining the types of accommodations that are reasonable to help you achieve optimum performance at work. *Read Chapter 12 carefully before you decide whether to disclose your ADHD to your employer in order to request accommodations.*

Note

1 Myers-Briggs Type Indicator www.myersbriggs.org.

This chapter will guide you through a self-analysis of the difficulties you are experiencing in your current job so you can carefully assess what degree of change you need to make to find more satisfaction at work—from seeking changes in your current position to changing jobs or even changing careers.

4

Problem Solving When You Need a Change at Work

Maybe you can't keep up with the demands of your job, or your boss is a nitpicker and reprimands you for being five minutes late, even though you work past quitting time on most days. Maybe you are expected to do the work of two people because your company hasn't replaced the last two colleagues that have departed. Or your boss wants you to be nothing but a rubber stamp and have no opinions of your own. There are lots of workplace situations that can build up and become unbearable over time. Don't give in to ADHD impulsivity. It may feel satisfying in the moment to say "I quit!" but after that fleeting moment has passed, you face unemployment and will need to explain why you can't use your last boss as a reference. Not a situation you want to be in! Instead, be strategic. Think of the long run and don't let yourself be tempted by that intense urge to resign without planning what's next.

Don't Throw the Baby Out with the Bathwater!

When you need a change, start small and then think bigger if the small changes don't help.

1. **First, consider a transfer within your current organization—** First, explore the possibility of a transfer within your organization. If your work is satisfying but your boss is impossible, a lateral move may be all you need.
2. **If that's not a possibility, consider seeking a similar job in another organization.** If a different position within your organization is not possible, the next step is to look for a similar job in another organization.
3. **A third-level possibility is to consider a different job in the same general field** that will use some of the skills you've developed while giving you the opportunity to learn new ones.
4. **Consider updating or enhancing your job skills.** Sick of your current job or boss? Look into the possibility of taking classes to upgrade or update your skills. Many employers will pay for such classes when they are related to your job.
5. **Consider earning a higher degree in your field while continuing to work at a less-than-ideal job.**
6. **As a last resort, consider a complete career change**—which may mean taking a lower-level job in a new field until you accumulate knowledge and experience. Alternatively, it may mean earning a certificate or degree in a new field.

So, now that I've outlined a ladder of choices, from least change to greatest change, let's go back to step one—what can be improved in your current job?

Improve Communication with Your Boss

Maybe you can improve your relationship with your supervisor by initiating more frequent communication. Many adults with ADHD communicate less and less as things start to go wrong. Then, when your supervisor asks why a certain project is behind schedule, you are left in a defensive position, needing to explain all that has gone wrong. If you've been in communication frequently, your boss will already know your progress has been held back because others on the project haven't sent you what you need or the manpower just isn't sufficient to get the job done on time. The more you stay in communication and engage in problem solving with your boss, the less likely your boss will be to blame all the problems on you.

Suggest reasonable accommodations that can help you work more efficiently. Work with an ADHD counselor/coach to identify workplace conditions that impede your progress. Would it help to work from home one day per week to allow time to concentrate and complete reports? Would it help to work more collaboratively on a project with someone else on the team whose strengths complement yours? Would it help to schedule weekly check-ins with your boss that will provide you with accountability and support?

Suggest Assignment to Projects That Are a Better Match for Your Strengths

Supervisors aren't mind readers and don't necessarily know which team member is best assigned to a particular task. Let your boss know what you're good at and like to do. Many adults I've worked with have been able to gradually reshape their job so that it is a better match for them—a win for both the employee and employer.

When You Have Concluded That You Need to Leave

Work with a job coach and look for a different job in a systematic way. Some adults with ADHD look for a new job in a sporadic, unfocused way. If you've had a particularly bad day at the office, do you come home fuming and get online that evening to look for a new job? When things settle down a bit, does your job search fall off until the next crisis occurs?

Instead of looking in a haphazard, emotion-driven fashion, use your job coach to keep you on track. Often I will ask people I work with to send me copies of the job descriptions of positions they want to apply to. That way, we can consider together whether the new position seems like a good job match. Sending these job postings to me increases accountability and provides structure so the job search continues in a consistent way.

Work with a job coach to consider a different type of work that still falls within your experience and training. If you and your job coach have concluded that the types of tasks required in your current job are not a good match with your temperament, skills, or interests.

Leaving Management Behind May Be Your Key to Success

Perhaps you have been promoted to a management position but find that keeping track of others and supervising them is not a strength of yours. It happens frequently that someone with ADHD shows talent in their job and then is promoted to a supervisory position in which they no longer do what they are good at. Instead, they are supervising others that perform those tasks. As a supervisor, much more paperwork, planning, and keeping track of others is required. Frequently, a supervisory position is frustrating for a talented adult with ADHD who would much rather dive into a task, hyperfocus, and not look up for hours. Instead, they are expected to prepare reports, attend tedious meetings, and keep track of everyone else while never getting to do the work itself. If you are struggling in a supervisory position, make an ADHD-friendly decision to move to a job that allows you to work at your best.

Jim was a highly skilled network engineer. Because he was intelligent, articulate, and hardworking, the management team in his company tapped him for a supervisory position. Jim was very pleased—that is until the reality of the new job began to sink in. Not only did he have his own projects to complete, but he now was expected to mentor and supervise a team of five junior colleagues. Because Jim was a self-starter, he naively assumed supervision would be a piece of cake—just describe the projects, assign tasks, and wait for them to be completed. As deadlines were missed and misunderstandings arose, Jim began to feel frustrated and overwhelmed. His first performance review came with a warning. Six months later, Jim was asked to leave this position.

Jim was devastated. He had always been a rising star until he was promoted to a management position. Working with an ADHD career counselor, Jim came to realize that he hadn't really liked the work of a supervisor; he'd just liked the title and the raise. He identified the things he had to offer and the types of tasks he excelled at and went searching for a job that would suit his skills. In short order, he was offered a job as a senior network consultant for a large international firm. Jim loved the international travel and stimulation of his new position, for which he was expected to jump on a plane, analyze a problem, and solve it in short order. Thriving in his new position, Jim looked back on his management job as one he wouldn't have taken had he thought it through with a job coach.

Think about an "Evolving" Job Instead of an Abrupt Job Change

While some people make abrupt, distinct job changes, for many other people, their career is a process of evolution.

One young man with ADHD began his adult life as a rock musician. He actually achieved some measure of success for a few years but tired of the hectic, stressful life. He quit performing and began earning a living recording other groups and renting practice and recording space.

As his siblings began having children, he became very involved with his nephews and nieces and began writing humorous children's songs for them. They were such a hit in the family that he began performing in local public schools. He developed a second performing career that did not entail the rugged performance schedule of a rock musician.

In his second performance career, he met a young teacher with whom he fell in love and married. She became the director of a childcare center. His open schedule allowed him much free time. He began playing at the childcare center, found he loved the work with children, and eventually decided to go back to school to study early childhood education. The songs he had written for children were of great interest to the school of education he attended and became the subject of his senior project. Ten years after he dropped out of college to pursue his rock music, his career has evolved very naturally, and in stages, into a radically different but even more satisfying career.

Don't Let Yourself Become Paralyzed by Choice!

Remember, you're not making a choice for *forever,* you're making a choice for right now. Ask yourself "What do I want to do next?" instead of "What do I want to do for the rest of my life?" Think of making a move to something better than your current job rather than making the *perfect* choice. Your needs and priorities will change over the course of your life. At certain times—when you have young children, for example—priorities such as a short commute may be high on your list. Later you may feel the freedom to accept a job that entails travel. At certain times, your priorities may lead you to select a part-time position; at other times you may need to maximize your income because you have children close to college age.

Finding the right fit is often an ongoing *process* through which you learn and grow, not a single *choice* you make with consequences you must live with forever. So go ahead, take the plunge. Look for a job that can move you more in the direction you'd like to head, even if it isn't the perfect long-term setting.

What If People Tell Me I'm Unrealistic in What I Want?

Some people settle for so little in their work lives. Jobs are certainly work and not play, but looking for a place where we can truly be comfortable and truly apply our gifts is a great pleasure and satisfaction in life. Finding a job that is interesting is even more essential when you have ADHD. You can't expect perfection, but neither should you be talked out of looking for real job satisfaction.

Don't let people who don't understand ADHD convince you that you're wrong in your reactions. ADHD is a very "reactive" disorder. Some workplace factors, which can be fairly easily accommodated or overlooked by others, may be truly intolerable to someone with ADHD. Your reactions may be entirely valid for you, even though they greatly differ from the reactions of others. Many people with ADHD are highly sensitive to distractions such as noise level, clutter, fluorescent lighting, emotional discord, interruptions, and stress. It is well worth your while, and not a self-indulgence, to look for a work environment that is your brand of ADHD friendly.

Give yourself permission to actively seek a work environment in which you can flourish. Taking responsibility for yourself and your life choices doesn't mean you expect the world to accommodate your every whim. If people tell you hardly any of us find the "perfect job," they're right. But having a thorough understanding of your needs, preferences, desires, strengths, and foibles can be enormously helpful, both in your current job and in any job you seek in the future. Knowing your needs doesn't mean you'll find a job that meets all of them, but you're much less likely to find a good job match if you don't even understand what your needs are!

Don't Lose Sight of What You Really Love to Do!

When you have ADHD, *doing what you love* is probably the best recipe of all for success. I don't mean this in some idealistic, impractical sense, but I want to emphasize the enormous importance of *motivation* for adults with ADHD in overcoming their other difficulties and hurdles. There is no greater motivation than doing what you really *want* to do!

Thinking about what types of work would truly satisfy you should be an ongoing process through which you learn and grow. What is best for you will almost certainly change as you go through your work life. Don't let yourself be frightened or paralyzed by choices or changes. Each change is rarely permanent but rather is just the next step in an evolving career.

If you feel miserable and unhappy in your current job, work with an ADHD counselor or coach so you can clearly understand the sources of your unhappiness. Is it the work itself? Is it unfair management practices? Do you find yourself frequently in conflict with your supervisor? Or are you simply bored and want a change? Start with problem solving. The most rapid positive change may be to look for ways to change your current situation.

There are other books that may be helpful to you in considering your options. One recent, very unconventional and highly received career guide is *Roadmap: The Get-It-Together Guide for Figuring Out What to*

Do with Your Life.[1] While not specifically for those with ADHD, many with ADHD will relate to *The Career Guide for Creative and Unconventional People.*[2] Other books that do not focus specifically on ADHD issues but that explore career lifestyle alternatives are *The Pathfinder,*[3] *Making a Living Without a Job,*[4] *Do What You Love, The Money Will Follow,*[5] and the career search classic already mentioned, *What Color Is Your Parachute?*[6]

Notes

1 Roadtrip Nation and Brian McAllister. (2015). *Roadmap: The Get-It-Together Guide for Figuring Out What to Do With Your Life.* San Francisco, CA: Chronicle Books.
2 Eickleberry, Carol. (2010). *The Career Guide for Creative and Unconventional People.* Berkeley, CA: Ten Speed Press.
3 Lore, Nicholas. (2012). *The Pathfinder: How to Choose or Change your Career for a Lifetime of Satisfaction and Success.* New York, NY: Touchstone Books.
4 Winter, Barbara. (2010). *Making a Living Without a Job, revised edition: Winning Ways for Creating Work That You Love.* New York, NY: Random House, LLC.
5 Sinetar, Marsha. (2015). *Do What you Love, the Money will Follow: Discover Your Right Livelihood.* Santa Rosa, CA: Sinetar and Associates.
6 Bolles, Richard. (2015). *What Color is Your Parachute? 2015: A Practical Manual for Job Hunters and Career-Changers.* Berkley, CA: Ten Speed Press.

This chapter explains the use of the Myers-Briggs Type Indicator (MBTI) to understand the interaction of personality and ADHD and to help you make career choices based on your personality type as it interacts with your ADHD traits.

5

ADHD and Personality Type at Work

ADHD Is *Not* a Personality Type!

Just as people with ADHD come in all shapes and sizes, they also come in all personality types. Certainly, people with ADHD have a number of traits in common, but even when you are only considering ADHD traits while ignoring personality traits, there is tremendous variety among people with ADHD. You may have had the experience of reading books on ADHD that described you to a tee. These books are describing the ADHD traits that many adults with ADHD have in common, traits you recognize in yourself. But it is important to realize that these books only address ADHD traits and ignore non–ADHD personality traits.

Some adults with ADHD are talkative extroverts, while others are quiet and private. They range from hyperactive to virtual couch potatoes, with some vacillating between the two. Some are highly impulsive, while others tend to be vague and indecisive. Some are highly intellectual, while others gravitate toward more active pursuits. What all these people share in common is some combination of core symptoms of ADHD. In this chapter, I will focus on individual personality differences among people with ADHD and discuss how those differences interact with certain ADHD traits to influence good career choices and functioning at work.

Although your ADHD symptoms may play an important role in your life, you are much more complex than a list of ADHD symptoms. By taking a measure of your personality traits and thinking about them in combination with your ADHD, you will have a more complete picture of your strengths, weaknesses, interests, and preferences. Taking all these factors into account, you will be much better able to find a good job or career match for yourself.

The Myers-Briggs Type Indicator (MBTI)[1] is a useful tool for assessing basic personality traits. Until recently, very little attention was paid to the MBTI in connection with ADHD. Although there is now growing interest in the uses of the MBTI with ADHD, only limited research exists. What is written in this chapter is based on my clinical experience over many years, observing how MBTI personality preferences interact with ADHD. If you are seeking to understand what would be a good job match or career match for yourself, knowledge of your MBTI personality type can be essential to making wise career decisions.

A Little about the MBTI

The Myers-Briggs Type Indicator (MBTI) is a commonly used measure of personality type. It is brief, widely available, and has been studied extensively in relation to job satisfaction and career match.[2] The MBTI is preferable to many other psychological tests of personality because it examines personality preferences, not personality problems. Most other "personality tests" are designed to identify pathology, while the MBTI is designed to look at personality characteristics in the general population.

The MBTI was developed based on the personality theory of the well-known psychoanalyst Carl Jung, who believed that individuals have inborn traits that form the basic building blocks of their personalities.[3]

Jung believed that these traits are fundamental and lifelong, but can develop and change in certain respects. Interestingly, as neuroscientists learn more about the neurobiological basis for personality traits, we are now beginning to see scientific evidence to support Jung's belief that people are born with different personality traits or tendencies.

Understanding MBTI "Preferences"

According to the MBTI, people vary along four dimensions of opposing "preferences." While all of us have some traits at both ends of each of the four dimensions, Jung believed we have a "preference" for one over the other. Some of us can be extreme in one or more dimension, while others fall near the midline, with a close balance of traits on either side.

Extroverted	(E)	or	Introverted	(I)
Sensing	(S)	or	Intuitive	(N)
Thinking	(T)	or	Feeling	(F)
Judging	(J)	or	Perceiving	(P)

Let's take a look at each of these eight preferences and how they are defined according to the MBTI.[4]

Extroversion/Introversion

Extroverts (Es) are people who are energized by interaction with others and actively seek their company. Being around people is life's blood for the extrovert. People who are strongly extroverted may feel lonely and isolated when forced to engage in solitary activities for prolonged periods on the job. They often prefer verbal over written communication, and they seek discussions with others in making decisions. They tend to relate to a broad range of people instead of maintaining only a few in-depth relationships. Extroverts are social and are oriented toward the external world—they live in a world of "we."

In contrast, introverts (Is) inhabit a more private, internal world. Introverts tend to recharge or reenergize themselves in isolation, away from others. Social interaction, especially with groups or with people who are not intimates, is energy draining for introverts. Although a certain amount of interaction is necessary within the course of a day, introverts are prone to close the office door, to wish the meeting were over, to turn off the telephone, and to want to leave the party early. Their energy level becomes depleted after prolonged interaction with others.

Let's look at some basic differences between Es and Is.

Differing Problem-Solving Styles between Es and Is

Introverts are prone to turn inward when making a decision and to announce their decision to others after they have reached their own conclusion. Even when engaged in problem solving with others, an introvert is likely to mull things over before discussing the matter. By contrast, many extroverts begin to develop their ideas as they engage in discussion and dialogue with others. For extroverts, the very act of communicating with others often sparks ideas that haven't yet occurred to them.

Cultural Bias toward Extroverts

In the United States, in particular, there seems to be a strong cultural bias toward extroversion. (Introverts not only have to face this social bias against their type but also find themselves outnumbered 3 to 1 in the general population.) Introverts may be seen as withdrawn or lacking in social skills. Because of this cultural preference toward extroversion, many introverts (intentionally or not) try to respond to the MBTI as if they were extroverts. In fact, many introverts spend most of their lives attempting to behave in an extroverted fashion, trying to suppress introverted tendencies.

For example, one business executive who answered the MBTI as an extrovert protested when his examiner suggested that he was more likely an introvert; he insisted that he was seen as a genial, outgoing person at work. This "I in E clothing" made the mistake many people do, namely, confusing extroversion with social skills. Like many introverts, he had developed excellent social skills. He was well liked and was highly regarded as an executive. Unlike a true extrovert, however, he tended to yearn for time when he could close his office door to get some work done, and he typically spent his evenings in quiet isolation to recover from his energy-draining, people-filled day.

Appreciating the Powers of Introversion

If you are an introvert, understand your "I" tendencies and celebrate them! Don't try to join the Es of the world in the erroneous assumption that introversion is something to change or hide. Is who try to force themselves into the shoes of an E won't enjoy walking and will probably get blisters! Accepting your introversion will lead to a much more satisfactory choice of career. It is the Is of the world who are able to sit and focus in order to write, create, learn, invent, and accomplish.

An extrovert relies on voicemail to avoid missing a call.

An introvert relies on voicemail to screen calls he might prefer to miss.

Sensing/Intuition

Just as the majority of people are extroverts, most people (approximately 75% of the population) have a preference for sensing (relating to things you can see, hear, touch, smell, and feel) as opposed to a preference for intuition, that is, thinking about abstract ideas.[5] Ss, those who prefer sensation, live in the world of practicality, whereas those who prefer intuition, the Ns, live in the domain of ideas and abstractions. Another way to express this difference is to say that Ss live in the world of the physical while Ns focus on ideas.

Ss Emphasize Hands-On Experience

Ss place the strongest emphasis on their experience, on what has actually happened. The nickname for Missouri—the "Show Me" State—must have been inspired by a group of Ss. Just like Missourians, Ss want to be shown the actual proof of things. They trust their own experience and pay the greatest attention to their surroundings, noticing details, collecting facts, and making concrete plans. Because Ss live in the world of things, they are natural-born shoppers. An S will likely read the newspaper ads for sales and will be the best source of information on where something can be bought for the best price.

Ns Live in the World of Ideas

Ns, on the other hand, live intuitively; they think of grand schemes, of possibilities, of the future. Ns are attuned to the creative, the imagined, the not yet actual. For an S, the Ns of the world may seem a bit flighty and impractical, dreamers who are always off in the clouds, who ignore the day-to-day requirements of life. Ns in turn may view Ss as unimaginative, plodding, and aware only of the boring, repetitive daily grind. Of course, there are people that are close to the midpoint on the S–N factor, people that are good at figuring out how things work but who also have creative ideas about how things could work—these S/Ns are the inventors of the world.

Ss and Ns Form a Powerful Team

Ss often make good planners and managers; they pay attention to the details of what has occurred and what needs to be taken care of next. Ns make good creators, visionaries. A company with an N at the helm will always be moving toward the future, developing innovations, seeking new markets, and expanding in unexpected directions. The actual execution of these grand schemes is best carried out by Ss, however. A company with an S at the helm will be more solid and practical, with an eye on the bottom line and on competitors, but with little sense of direction other than an impulse to continue to do whatever it has done best in the past.

Of all the contrasts between personality preferences, the S–N difference is considered the greatest. It is almost as if Ss and Ns speak different languages and have difficulty translating from one to the other. However, if this translation succeeds—if the two can learn to work together, respecting and understanding their differences—an S and an N can prove to be an unbeatable team!

An N expands life's possibilities.
An S makes the possible actual.

Thinking/Feeling

Thinkers (Ts) approach decisions from a somewhat detached, analytical, logical position. They value justice perhaps more highly than compassion. Feelers (Fs), on the other hand, make decisions in a more subjective manner, responding with empathy and trying to consider extenuating circumstances. For example, when someone has broken a rule, a T is likely to impose a standard penalty, whereas an F would, by reflex, consider the circumstances that led to the infraction. The T might say, "He has to pay the price for what he has done," but an F might say, "Yes, but he's never done anything like this before, and he was under tremendous stress when this happened."

T/F Gender Differences

This thinker–feeler dichotomy is the only set of preferences that shows a slight gender-related bias: Approximately 60% of women are Fs, whereas approximately 60% of men are Ts.[6] Ts and Fs can work together with great complementarity inasmuch as good decision making requires that both the thinking and the feeling aspects of a question be considered. Of course, we are all capable of considering both T and F aspects of questions, but people generally tend to have a preference in one direction or the other.

People versus Production

Both Ts and Fs are capable of experiencing strong emotional reactions to events, but since Fs are more likely to openly show their emotions, they are usually seen as warmer and more compassionate than Ts. The higher you go in the management hierarchy of an organization, the more likely you are to be a T. It may be that T qualities are necessary to guard the interests of the organization against the multiple competing needs of the employees. The T keeps an ever-vigilant eye on the bottom line. It may be just as true, however, that Fs are rare in upper-management jobs because such positions of leadership, which are so detached from personal involvement with people, are less attractive to them.

Ts think with their heads.
Fs think with their hearts.

Judging/Perceiving

The words "judging" and "perceiving" can be easily misinterpreted. It is a common error to think that "judging" means "to be judgmental." A better way of distinguishing judgers (Js) from perceivers (Ps) is to think of the difference between "defined" and "open-ended." Js are result oriented and want to get the job done, to make a plan, to meet the deadline. Ps, on the other hand, don't see the same value or urgency in accomplishing work. They feel much more strongly that work should be enjoyable, and they are likely to seek ways to avoid those tasks that are not enjoyable.

Deadlines

One of the most observable differences between Js and Ps can be seen in their responses to deadlines. For Js, a deadline is a serious limit that should be met. Js meet deadlines and expect their coworkers to meet them as well. For Ps, a deadline is seen as a marker that can slide. For some Ps, a deadline can even be seen as a signal to begin a project rather than a time to complete it! (This P preference can easily be mistaken for the procrastination patterns found in adults with ADHD. However, there is an important difference: Whereas Ps prefer to operate in that fashion, many adults with ADHD feel almost helpless to work against their tendency to procrastinate and feel frustrated by the pattern.)

Decisions

Another major difference can be found in decision making. Js, who like order, plans, and closure, tend to feel a sense of unease or agitation until a decision is made. "Let's figure out what we're going to do and make a decision," a J would say. Once a decision is made, the J feels more relaxed and secure. This drive or sense of urgency to make decisions or to settle issues can sometimes lead to decisions that are made too quickly, without gathering enough information. Ps, by contrast, have a great tolerance for ambiguity and are quite comfortable considering all aspects of a question. Ps are always happy to wait before making a decision. "Who knows? Perhaps new options will emerge. What's the rush?" a P would say. Whereas a J feels relief after a decision is made, this type of closure often causes the opposite reaction in a P. "If we decide now, we may be closing off other options that could be better," a P might argue. "Why don't we just keep thinking, talking, and gathering information a bit longer?"

**Js want plans to come together.
Ps want plans to hang loose.**

MBTI Types and Mistypes

In order for the MBTI to be useful, you will need to obtain an accurate measure of your MBTI personality type. You may have already taken the MBTI. Several million people take the MBTI each year. If you have taken it, the primary concern is whether you received an accurate measure of your type. If you are correctly typed, the MBTI can be enormously informative and useful in considering career concerns.

The reader should be aware that it is quite possible to take the MBTI and receive incorrect results. One man spoke with great mistrust of the MBTI, saying that he had taken it several times and had received a different personality type each time. How is this possible? The MBTI is simply a way of organizing and interpreting your self-report. "Garbage in, garbage out" is the rule that applies. To be "typed" correctly, you must answer questions according to your true preferences, not according to how you think you ought or how you try to be. People may be typed incorrectly if they have a job or lifestyle that requires them to behave very differently than they would naturally choose to behave. To be accurately typed, you must respond to the MBTI according to your true inclinations, even though the demands of your daily life may require you to behave otherwise.

Ideally, your type should be "verified" by a counselor or professional trained in interpreting the MBTI. One exercise I often find useful is to read a description of the personality type that results from an individual's answers. If they identify strongly with that description, their type is most likely correct. Often, however, if scores are near the midline on one of the four dimensions, the true type may lie across the line with the opposite preference. For example, if someone is very close to the middle between being a T and an F, I read two personality type descriptions with all other dimensions remaining the same—such as ENFP versus ENTP. Usually, you will recognize yourself much more strongly in one of the two personality types.

Mistyping in the Business World

People who take the MBTI as part of a workplace exercise may consciously or unconsciously answer questions in accordance with the values of the institution or in response to perceived social pressures. For example, some people in the business world may feel pressured to behave in an extroverted fashion even though by nature they are more private. Moreover, men in general (and perhaps especially those in the business world) may feel a strong social pressure to be logical rather than emotional. Thus, men who are truly feelers may respond to questions on the MBTI in a way that types them as thinkers, just as true introverts may respond in a way that types them as extroverts. Moreover, as women make efforts to reach upper-level management, those who are feelers may also be tempted to misrepresent themselves as thinkers.

Mistyping in Periods of Personal Change

Another source of mistyping can occur when a person is in counseling or is going through a midlife crisis, a divorce, a career change, or any other major life transition. These are all generally situations of internal turmoil and change. During such times, people may try to "become" different. As they experiment with different ways of feeling and responding, they may answer the MBTI accordingly.

Do Personality Types Change?

According to Jungian theory, our basic personality preferences are inborn and don't change throughout our lifetime.[7] This does not mean that we cannot make changes or improvements in ourselves. In fact, many people in their middle years begin to develop other aspects of their personality. For example, extroverts may begin to develop more solitary activities. Thinkers who have spent their careers focusing on the impersonal world of things may begin to learn how to express their emotions more openly. These changes are healthy and result in a more balanced life, but they don't result in a basic change in personality type. The situation is a bit like that of right-handed people who learn to eat with their left hands; although they can learn to do it, they will continue to have a strong preference for their right hands.

MBTI Preferences versus ADHD Tendencies

Now that you have a basic understanding of MBTI preferences, let's think about how those preferences interact with ADHD traits. When Carl Jung developed his theory of personality, he attempted to describe inborn personal preferences. According to Jung, each individual is born with these preferences and is most natural and comfortable in life when he or she behaves in accordance with those preferences. This set of preferences should not be confused with behavior patterns or tendencies associated with ADHD. ADHD traits do not exist due to personal preferences. In fact, more often, ADHD traits such as forgetfulness or disorganization are far from preferred. Instead, they are considered undesirable. Similarly, a person can have a strong tendency to stutter, but he or she is unlikely to have a preference for stuttering. The same kind of distinction can be made for many ADHD traits—they may be a tendency but not a preferred way of being.

It's easy to confuse preferences (the way we naturally prefer to be) with tendencies (the way we actually act on a daily basis). This difference is very important when ADHD is part of the picture. For example, if your personality type includes a J, your strong *preference* may be to make plans and be organized, but your ADHD may make it difficult to behave according to your *preference* for order and timeliness. It's also possible, if your personality type contains a P, that you may be mistaken for having ADHD when you don't—because Ps have a preference to avoid plans and final decisions. Interestingly, a study of several hundred schoolchildren found that the MBTI personality types that might be mistaken for ADHD were found slightly more often among *non-ADHD* students than among those with ADHD![8] The take-away message is that

ADHD traits do not constitute a personality type, and many that seem to have an "ADHD personality type" may not have ADHD at all.

Although people with ADHD come in all personality types, it is certainly possible for them to have personality preferences that are congruent with certain ADHD traits. When personality preferences and ADHD tendencies coincide, the result is an intensification of both! Double trouble!

ADHD strategies must fit your personality type.

How Do ADHD Traits and MBTI Preferences Interact at Work?

Let's examine how MBTI preferences interact with ADHD patterns, focusing on the workplace environment.

Extroverts (Es) with ADHD

If an extrovert falls on the hyperactive end of the ADHD continuum, he or she is likely to be hypertalkative and hypersocial. During school years, it's likely that he or she was constantly talking in class. Because an extroverted hyperactive individual is drawn to interact with others, people are likely to be one of life's major distractions. Extroverts (Es) are drawn to people to recharge, to discuss, and to problem solve. When an E also has ADHD, discussions are at risk to wander off the track, extend in time, and lose their effectiveness.

When People Are a Distraction, the Solution Needs to Be "E friendly"

Solutions for ADHD–related problems need to be modified to suit MBTI preferences. For example, one E with ADHD was highly distracted by conversations and by people walking by in the hall near his office. His therapist suggested that he shut his office door periodically to decrease these distractions. Because the man was such a strong E, this solution was unworkable for him. With his door shut, he found that his productivity became even worse! He felt isolated and was so curious about the bits and snatches of conversation he could overhear through his closed door that these conversations became even more distracting than before. A much more effective solution for him was to "time-shift" his hours. He began arriving at work at 7:30 a.m., which allowed him an hour or more of uninterrupted time to do paperwork, check e-mail, and organize his day before his coworkers began arriving.

Work That Is Isolating Can Become Intolerable for an E with ADHD

One woman with ADHD trained as a research chemist. She found the science fascinating, but once she was out of school, away from the interaction with fellow students, she found herself miserable on the job, where she was expected to work quietly, with little or no interaction with others for long stretches. After much thought, she reached the conclusion that she was significantly mismatched with her career path. She considered a number of professions that involved more people interaction and ultimately chose to go into real estate sales, a profession in which she found both success and satisfaction.

Turning Others Off by Hypertalking

Es with ADHD need to guard against talking too much at work. One man who sold technical equipment found that his major problem in sales was talking his client's ear off. He made some progress in checking this tendency by making brief notes of the points he wanted to make before calling each client. For initial calls, he developed a script that helped keep him on track but with which he allowed himself some latitude. He also used timers and set the goal of limiting client calls to 10 minutes. Most challenging of all, he learned to ask questions and then stop to listen to the answers. With all of these strategies in place, he became a much more effective salesperson.

Put Your Drive to Interact with Others to Work for You

Es may tend to prolong meetings, to socialize at the water fountain, and to infringe on the time of others because of their hunger for interaction. If you are an E with ADHD, you are even more likely to become caught up in such nonproductive behavior and may be misperceived by your boss or coworkers as a goof-off. If you are always seeking out the company of others, which takes you away from your work, consider shifting to a job that *requires* people interaction. This same energy and drive to socialize, which can be seen as work avoidance in some jobs, can become your greatest asset in a people-oriented job.

Introverts (Is) with ADHD

What happens when someone with ADHD is an introvert? If you are an I with ADHD, you may feel an internal conflict between your desire to work alone and your need for structure provided by coworkers or supervisors. If you have ADHD and are isolated for significant portions of each day, it is quite easy to drift off the track or spend far too much time on a particular task without realizing that this has taken place. One introvert (I) with ADHD learned to cue himself to keep on track. He set concrete goals at the beginning of each day and estimated an approximate time period for each task. He then found it helpful to set a timer to sound every half hour as a cue to check his focus and his progress.

Prefer to Communicate in Writing

E-mail is a wonderful mode of communication for Is. One I with ADHD found that it was helpful to communicate frequently with his boss by e-mail as a means of building structure and receiving feedback. He set weekly goals for himself and sent them to his boss (down the hall) by e-mail. At the end of each week, he e-mailed his boss a progress report.

They met face to face twice monthly. E-mail allowed him to minimize direct interaction but, at the same time, to benefit from external structure and guidance.

Stress Sensitive

Is report that they frequently feel overwhelmed by too many interruptions or too much verbal interaction. They become flooded or overwhelmed with stimulation to the point that they shut down. Again, e-mail can provide a solution to such flooding, because it can allow efficient communication without overloading the verbal interaction circuits. Some Is with ADHD have carefully arranged to work at night to avoid overstimulation. One I with ADHD, who was very sensitive to stress and overstimulation, arranged his workday so that he could arrive home before rush hour and complete phone calls and paperwork from the peace and quiet of his home.

Sensers (Ss) with ADHD

What happens when those who prefer sensation (Ss) have ADHD? Ss are practical, active, and focused on the world of things. An S with ADHD may be especially prone to start far too many projects and to constantly find himself in the midst of long-standing uncompleted renovations and repairs. An S with ADHD may shop compulsively or may pick up many hobbies, which they drop as they pursue their next interest. They are likely to buy all the latest equipment for each new hobby, only to leave all these acquisitions in disarray as they move on to something else.

Surrounded by Things

How do Ss with ADHD tend to function at work? The same patterns can be found at work as at home: a tendency toward great physical disorder, toward the acquisition of too many things, and toward impulsive spending and unrealistic budgeting. Ss with ADHD are the inventors of the world; they are constantly tinkering, building, adding on. These tendencies can be a great asset if they are managed, but all too often, Ss with ADHD live surrounded by objects only partially completed or repaired.

Lost in the Details

Ss with ADHD may be especially prone to become lost in the details of a project. For example, one man decided to make improvements in the Day-Timer system he used to help him plan and organize. He became completely engrossed in this project, developing special color coding systems, huge computer printouts, and intricate systems of symbols, meanwhile never putting his time-management program into effect. Ss with ADHD often need a non–ADHD colleague to help them reach closure. When they are teamed with someone who can provide boundaries and limits, their practical solutions can be quite creative and valuable to the organization.

Intuitives (Ns) with ADHD

People who prefer intuition (Ns) and who also have ADHD have the potential to be among the most creative and prolific people in the world—if their energy and interests can be harnessed. Ns live in the world of theories, ideas, and innovations. Unlike the innovations of their S counterparts, the innovations of Ns are not of the concrete "build a better mousetrap" variety but are more likely to concern the abstract themes of art, philosophy, educational theory, or government policy. Ns with ADHD often report that they live with a flood of ideas and associations and that they tend to be highly distracted by their own internal world.

Drowning in a Sea of Ideas

One N with severe ADHD, a highly intelligent man, reported with enormous frustration that he wanted to write a book for others like himself but found that he couldn't organize and develop his thoughts. Although he had developed a huge list of random thoughts and associations over the course of several years of intense effort, he was unable to combine these into a format he could communicate to others. Another N with ADHD, a man whose organizational problems were less severe, described his professional life as very satisfying but constantly stressful. He found that he was interested in a huge range of topics and was unable to realistically assess the demands of his current commitments before taking on another tempting project. As an adult with ADHD, he also struggled with procrastination and invariably put off papers and reports until the last minute.

Visionaries in Need of a Plan

In the workplace, Ns can be great leaders and visionaries. However, an N with ADHD at the helm of an organization is likely to lead the entire organization into his or her world of unrealistic plans, overcommitment, and frequent crises created by poor planning and procrastination. Team up such an N with a non–ADHD S, and many more of his or her ideas will bear fruit!

Thinkers (Ts) with ADHD

When ADHD occurs in those whose preferred style is for thinking over feeling (the Ts), the result is sometimes a combination of troubling interpersonal tendencies. Thinkers (Ts) prefer to deal with nonpeople issues: technology, profit, efficiency, or procedure. Their emotional, empathic side is much less developed. While some Ts may be good observers of human reactions, they are not prone to respond in a fashion that engenders closeness or mutual understanding. Many people with ADHD also have difficulty reading social cues and emotional responses. It is as if their engine is running so fast (i.e., they are so preoccupied with their own thoughts and activities) that there is little time or energy left over to expend on other people. When a thinking preference is combined with ADHD, problems with people skills can be doubly intensified.

Missing Social Cues

When ADHD traits of impatience and low frustration tolerance are combined with a T's lack of attention to the feelings of others, there may be significant interpersonal problems on the job. Such people may be both difficult to work for and difficult to manage or supervise. If they are extroverts, they may be especially prone to talk nonstop and to be oblivious to the effect they are having on others. If they are introverts, their attempts to escape from the demands of interpersonal interaction may make them respond to people in a way that suggests indifference or annoyance.

Need to Build Social Skills

Social skills are likely to be a major difficulty for Ts with ADHD. They will do well to team themselves closely with an F who can temper their reactions and can give them feedback about their effect on coworkers.

Feelers (Fs) with ADHD

Feelers (Fs) with ADHD are in a better position to develop good social skills. While Ts with ADHD have a doubly influenced tendency to misread or overlook social cues, Fs with ADHD have a tendency to be tuned in to the needs and feelings of others. This tendency gives Fs with ADHD the means to counteract some of the interpersonal problems sometimes caused by ADHD. For example, Fs with ADHD may still blurt out something in a blunt or undiplomatic fashion. Their built-in social radar, however, will quickly tell them that they have overstepped the bounds of considerate behavior, thus giving them an opportunity to apologize and to mend fences. One woman, an F with ADHD, reported that she was always having to "sweep up the pieces" after she had unintentionally upset someone. In fact, she consciously developed a charming, self-deprecating, and outgoing manner in order to compensate for unintentional faux pas.

Emotionality

Fs with ADHD may find that their emotional and interpersonal reactions are intense, because their ADHD traits toward overemotionality, combined with their emotional sensitivity, are likely not only to be aware of others' hurt feelings but to experience such feelings themselves. Some Fs with ADHD (more often female, though not always) may feel that they are on an emotional roller coaster, with strong tendencies toward tears, anxiety, and depression.

A T with ADHD may have fairly thick skin and may be somewhat oblivious to the negative reactions of others. Ts may have intense emotions of frustration, anger, or depression. If they have ADHD challenges related to impulse control, such Ts may become known in the workplace for overreacting with angry outbursts, showing little regard for the impact such outbursts have on others.

Intense Relationships

The emotional intensity of Fs with ADHD in combination with their social sensitivity may lead them to have intense intimate friendships and love relationships. This is in marked contrast to Ts with ADHD (more often male), who may be emotionally unavailable and may have relatively few relationships with others. Fs with ADHD, if well matched to their careers and jobs, can use their strong awareness of others to advantage in sales, public relations, and in any other type of work requiring people interaction and sensitivity. Stress can be the Achilles' heel for Fs with ADHD. During high stress, their heightened sensitivity to others may lead to overreactions and less effective functioning.

Judgers (Js) with ADHD

Judgers (Js) with ADHD are in a battle with themselves. Due to their strong *preference* for order, closure, and predictability, ADHD tendencies such as disorganization, poor time management, and forgetfulness are particularly stressful for them. The disorganization caused by their ADHD is at odds with their built-in preference for order. Their battle has both positive and negative consequences. If the resulting frustration is extreme, it can result in self-rejection, low self-esteem, and depression. If the frustration is mild, it can result in the development of effective coping techniques.

Tendency toward Rigidity

In extreme cases, Js with ADHD may develop patterns that can be misunderstood as obsessive-compulsive tendencies. In their attempt to gain control over their uncooperative ADHD brains, Js may develop numerous rituals and habits to which they adhere rigidly. When J tendencies and ADHD traits are both strong, the degree of rigidity may become extreme, causing problems for the J in living and working with others.

Js Often Compensate Well for ADHD

When J tendencies are less pronounced or when the ADHD traits are less severe, Js with ADHD have a great advantage over Ps in compensating for ADHD patterns. Often, even without the assistance of others, Js naturally develop behavior patterns or habits consisting of techniques to combat absentmindedness, cope with distractions, stay on schedule, meet deadlines, and so on. Typically, Js with ADHD eagerly adopt all the coping techniques that come to their attention, since suggestions to create and maintain order are highly compatible with their own internal drives. These drives constitute their great strength: If they can moderate their frustration and their negative evaluation of themselves when their ADHD breaks through, Js have a great capacity and desire to compensate for their ADHD.

Perceivers (Ps) with ADHD

Perceivers (Ps), on the other hand, can suffer from what might seem like an excess of comfort with their ADHD tendencies. The ADHD patterns of a P may be more irritating and troubling for those who live and work with them than for the Ps themselves. This is because Ps (with or without ADHD) by nature prefer to live in a less ordered, defined, predictable fashion. When their natural preference for spur-of-the-moment living is combined with the impulsivity of ADHD, a volatile combination can result. Unlike Js with ADHD, Ps have weak brakes and strong accelerators. Thus, Ps with ADHD may feel it is entirely justified to change plans at the last moment if they have just been inspired by a new idea or motivated by an impulse to do something more desirable. Their surroundings are likely to reflect the fact that they live at the highest level of chaos, with little or no organization among their papers and belongings. Often, Ps will remark that their chaos results from rushing ahead to the next appealing activity rather than taking time to plan or put things away.

Need for a Tolerant Environment

Ps with ADHD may experience more difficulty than other personality types in finding a workplace environment that can tolerate their disorganization while appreciating their gifts. One P with ADHD, for this very reason, started his own small advertising agency. Being the boss, he answered to no one. When his assistant arrived promptly at 8:30 each morning, she often found her boss asleep on the carpet, where he had crashed after working all night. Similarly, after working nonstop on a project, he felt free to take a day or two off, even midweek. By working for himself, he was able to create a work life that was compatible with his strong P tendencies to follow the ebb and flow of his energies. Many Ps with ADHD find themselves most at home in a creative environment, where it is the norm to work in spurts and at odd hours.

Need for Help with Structure

While Ps with ADHD can be tremendously creative, effective people, they (perhaps more than other ADHD adults) have great need of organized non–ADHD persons to help them maintain some degree of order in their work lives.

MBTI Personality Types

Through combining the eight basic preferences described in this chapter, the MBTI classifies a person according to sixteen personality types:

ISTJ	ISFJ	INFJ	INTJ
ISTP	ISFP	INFP	INTP
ESTP	ESFP	ENFP	ENTP
ESTJ	ESFJ	ENFJ	ENTJ

I have talked in broad strokes about the eight preferences of the MBTI* and how these preferences may interact with ADHD. In reality, however, the picture is far more complex than this. Each person has four preferences, which interact with one another. ADHD traits complicate the issue even further. For example, an extroverted P with a preference toward feelings and an introverted P who is a logical, analytical thinker are going to be affected by their ADHD very differently.

It is far beyond the scope of this chapter—and could indeed be a book in itself—to talk of each personality type and its potential interaction with ADHD. There are many excellent books written on the subject of the Myers-Briggs Type Indicator. Reading these books, especially those with a focus on the MBTI and careers, and thinking of the ways that personality type and ADHD interact, which I have only touched upon in this chapter, can be helpful to you in making career choices or changes.

The most important message to take from this chapter is that you are much more than an adult with ADHD. It's very important to be aware of your ADHD traits and tendencies, but don't lose sight of the fact that you are unique and complex. Solutions to your ADHD problems need to be custom tailored to you, taking your personality preferences into consideration. Keeping your personality preferences in mind in combination with ADHD issues will help you make a choice that makes sense for you, not just for your ADHD!

Notes

1 Myers, I. B., & Briggs, K. C. (1976). *Myers-Briggs Type Indicator*. Palo Alto, CA: Consulting Psychologists Press.
2 Martin, C., & Sommer, E. (2009). *Looking at Type: Your Career*. Gainesville, FL: Center for Applications of Psychological Type, Inc.
3 Myers, I. B., & Myers, P. B. (2010). *Gifts Differing: Understanding Personality Type* Boston: Nicholas Brealey Publishers.
4 Keirsey, D. (1998). *Please Understand Me II: Temperament, Character, Intelligence.* Toronto, ON. Prometheus Nemesis Book Co.
5 Ibid.
6 Ibid.
7 Ibid.
8 Meisgeier, C., Poillion, M., & Haring, K. (1994). The relation between ADHD and Jungian psychological type: Commonality in Jungian psychological type preferences among students with Attention Deficit Hyperactivity Disorder. *Proceedings of the international symposium, Orchestrating Change in the 90s: The Role of Psychological Type*. Gainesville, FL.
* In several subsequent chapters, you will find many references to aspects of the MBTI. If you are not familiar with the MBTI, you may find it helpful to refer to this chapter and to read some of the books on the MBTI.

Attention deficit hyperactivity disorder is very often associated with other types of cognitive or learning differences. This chapter discusses ways to both identify and understand your learning differences and how they may affect you on the job.

6

ADHD and Learning Challenges

ADHD rarely exists in isolation. Learning differences very often accompany ADHD. If you are an adult, you may have mild to moderate learning disorders that were never identified during your school years. The most common learning disorders are in reading, writing, and math. You may also have challenges in processing verbal information so that you can clearly understand and recall it.

In the ADHD Workplace Questionnaire, you are asked to answer a short list of questions under the heading Related Cognitive Difficulties. Answering "yes" to a number of these problems may be an indication that you are dealing with specific learning differences in addition to attention issues. If you have a learning disorder, you may benefit from certain types of assistance and from accommodations on the job.

Why Should You Be Concerned about Learning Disorders at Work?

Our life as learners doesn't end with school days. The demands of the workplace are constantly changing, and with those changes comes the need to continually learn new tasks to keep pace with job requirements. For many of us, those changes include becoming more computer literate or a learning complicated new software systems. Learning disorders can have a profound impact on workplace training seminars. The training that takes place in government, commerce, and industry is not geared to accommodate the needs of people with learning disorders.

Until recently, there were more jobs for individuals who had difficulty with reading, writing, and mathematics. The majority of these hands-on jobs have been taken over by machines, and the demands for reading and writing have increased rather than decreased. As a result, it has become increasingly important to identify and help adults with learning disorders that may not have been identified until adulthood.

Coping with Learning Anxiety

One of the most difficult aspects of learning for adults with a history of learning problems is the anxiety they experience when they are placed in a situation that reminds them of their school days—that is, situations in which they are expected to read, write, or learn new material and to pass tests to demonstrate new learning.

Many adults, with or without learning differences, often experience intense anxiety when they are required to engage in public speaking, to rapidly learn new material in intensive training workshops, to quickly read and respond to written material, and to rapidly and efficiently produce written reports.

If you are placed in a new situation that reminds you of frustrating or embarrassing situations from your school years, you may experience a conditioned chain reaction that begins with discomfort, anxiety, or panic and leads to an inability to perform, feelings of shame, and a desire to escape, resulting in damaged self-esteem. Each time you go through a chain reaction like this, your fear of learning or performing is strengthened.

Overcoming your learning anxiety

You should undertake a number of active steps if learning anxiety is interfering with work performance.

Let Go of Your Negative Thinking

Many adults today who have learning disorders were never diagnosed as children and never received any special assistance. They grew up thinking of themselves as poor students or as not very smart. In recent years, as more and more adults have been identified with learning problems, many tutors and coaches have begun to specialize in working with adults who have learning problems.

Consider working with an adult tutor

Good tutors can help adults with learning disorders push past their fears and anxieties. When these adults begin to enjoy the challenge of learning and believe they can build their learning skills, they have already won more than half the battle. If you don't believe you can join the ranks of successful learners, take a peek at some of the success stories at the end of this chapter. All of those whose stories I share with you had a long history of academic struggles and failure before they began their learning adventures in adulthood.

Seek an Evaluation of Your Learning Problems

You need to understand exactly what you are dealing with if you have learning challenges. It is increasingly common for adults who were never evaluated for learning problems during childhood to seek a diagnosis of their difficulties. A good LD evaluation should help you:

1. Pinpoint and clarify your specific learning problems
2. Outline a program to remediate your learning problems

3. Document your disorder, making you eligible for certain types of assistance

Several national organizations are dedicated to serving the needs of individuals with learning disorders. The Learning Disorder Association (LDA) is a large national organization that has active chapters in each state.[1] Through the LDA website, www.ldaamerica.org, you can gain information about state and local chapters. Your state chapter should be able to provide you with information about the services and organizations nearest you that offer both testing and tutoring support to help you minimize your learning problems.

Learning disorders don't go away, but that doesn't mean there is nothing you can do about them. There are many successful ways to cope with learning problems.

Common Workplace Difficulties for Adults with ADHD/LD

An adult with both ADHD and a learning disorder (LD) can encounter a variety of difficulties on the job. I have listed below some of the most common workplace learning challenges.

Slow Learning Curve

Some ADHD adults need significantly more repetitions than non–ADHD adults to learn a new task. If you tend to be slow in mastering new material, you will need to take this into account in job selection, avoiding organizations that tend to be pressured and fast paced and choosing one that will allow you to learn naturally, at your own pace. You should be careful not to let yourself be seduced by a higher-paying or more prestigious job whose demands will eventually overwhelm you.

If a training module at work goes too quickly, tell the trainer you need extra assistance. Ask permission to record training modules in order to review them later. Arrange for extra time to learn new skills or procedures—even if it means temporarily working in the evening or on weekends. For particularly difficult learning situations, you may need to arrange for individual training that can go at your pace until you master the material.

Difficulty in Processing Verbal Information

Prolonged listening is a problem for many ADHD adults. For some, this is a function of inattention and distractibility. Their ability to concentrate while receiving auditory information is limited; attention begins to wander, and essential information is missed.

For other ADHD adults, listening difficulties are compounded by an auditory processing problem that makes it difficult to receive, process, and comprehend oral input. Because processing spoken language is difficult, they become rapidly fatigued during prolonged meetings, conferences, and intensive training workshops. If an ADHD adult has difficulty with extended verbal interactions, he or she will generally function better doing work that can be done alone or in one-to-one interactive situations.

Review material in advance, if possible, prior to meetings. Information that is familiar to you will be easier to process while you're in the meeting.

Ask for assignments and work-related information to be sent to you in writing. When you have difficulty processing verbal information, it's important to ask to receive most communications in written format so that you can review them and refer to them as needed.

(story continued)
Consider using support technology that allows you to easily record lectures, meetings, and conversations. (See Chapter 16 for more information about audio notes.)

Writing Difficulties

Many ADHD adults make errors in the mechanics of written language—in spelling, punctuation, capitalization, and grammar—in part because of inattention to detail and impulsivity. When you struggle with planning and organization, this can also take a toll on writing ability, resulting in reports with run-on sentences, inadequate elaboration, muddled thinking, and poor organization. Many ADHD adults who are able to speak articulately find themselves struggling with written expression, because many more skills and abilities come into play when language is expressed in writing.

If writing is a major challenge for you, you should carefully investigate the extent to which writing is required on a job. On the other hand, if your writing difficulties are moderate, you should not automatically eliminate jobs that require writing. Computer programs now minimize the problems associated with the mechanics of writing, and the ease with which sentences can be deleted and paragraphs rearranged greatly aids the process of organizing a document. If you struggle with writing, taking far too long to write memos, e-mails, and reports, here are some things to consider:

Work intensively with a writing coach who specifically works with adults. Writing is a skill that is often not taught adequately during school years.

(story continued)

Look for someone to talk through your ideas (and record them!) before you start writing—you will probably feel more relaxed, and ideas will flow more easily when you are not simultaneously engaged in trying to write them in a clear, cogent, grammatically correct format while also paying attention to spelling and punctuation. Engaging in a back-and-forth discussion of the report, letter, e-mail, article, or web post will also be likely to trigger good ideas that may not have occurred to you working solo.

Consider using speech-to-text software (see Chapter 16 for more information). This type of software has been very well developed and, with only a little training, can accurately record your spoken word. Just as talking ideas through with someone can ease tension, talking to your computer can be an easy first step in getting your thoughts into written format.

Use software that helps you structure and develop your ideas (see Chapter 16). Recently, software has been developed that can provide a clear structure to each paragraph as well as to the document as a whole. You can create an outline using such software and then go back to populate each paragraph with an expanded discussion of your topic sentence.

Cognitive Fatigue

Some ADHD adults find their energy level rapidly depleted when engaging in any effortful mental activity. One kind of cognitive fatigue is specifically related to an area of learning disorder. It makes sense that when an activity is difficult for you, you will become cognitively fatigued rather quickly.

Another kind of cognitive fatigue occurs with any activity that calls for intense concentration. ADHD adults with this difficulty may be perceived by others as work avoiders owing to their frequent trips away from their desk to take breaks. Such individuals often report that they feel tired and sleepy while working but feel energetic as soon as they are up and moving around. For ADHD adults who struggle with mental fatigue, a job that allows more physical activity and fewer periods of prolonged concentration is often best.

Divide and conquer. In any job, there will be times when you are required to work in areas that are challenging. The more challenging a task, the more often you will need a break. So remember to divide and conquer—break the most difficult task into discrete chunks and deliberately move to less challenging work to give yourself a break from intense concentration.

Pay attention to times of day when you have the most energy and clarity of thought. Each of us tends to have rhythms—times of day when we can do our best work. Pay attention to that and plan to tackle your most challenging tasks during your best times of day.

Do aerobic exercise just before tackling a tough task. Research shows us that aerobic exercise causes our brains to start producing a neurochemical called BDNF (brain-derived neurotrophic factor) that enhances brain functioning. So exercise before work or exercise at lunch, and then tackle the tasks that need the greatest concentration.

Be sure your blood sugar level is steady. Thinking is hard work and requires adequate fuel. Instead of pumping yourself up with sugar and caffeine, eat protein at every meal to keep your blood sugar level steady throughout the day.

Should You Tell Anyone about Your Learning Disorder?

The same advice holds for learning disorders as for ADHD. There is widespread misunderstanding about learning disorders. An unenlightened employer may hear the term "learning disorder" or "LD" and assume you are not capable of performing your job or that you are below average in intellectual ability. The best approach is to find help in the areas where you need it and to ask for accommodations at work, where possible, without making a formal disclosure of your learning disorder.

There are circumstances, however, just as with ADHD, when it is to your advantage to disclose your learning disorder. For example:

1. When you have a supportive and sympathetic supervisor who will respond positively to your problem
2. When you have tried all other approaches, have found that you cannot do your job effectively without accommodations, and have not been able to obtain those accommodations without a formal disclosure
3. When you are in imminent danger of losing your job owing to problems related to your learning disorder and feel that with appropriate accommodations, you will be able to function well

Back to School with LD and/or ADHD

Documenting, understanding, and seeking help for a learning disorder is even more essential if you are planning to continue your education. A wide range of services is available to undergraduate, graduate, and professional students who have documented learning disorders. The documentation required is a learning disorder evaluation from a professional qualified to diagnose LD and ADHD.

If you are among the many adults with learning disorders or ADHD that experienced enormous difficulty in their school years and may have quit school as a result, it's important for you to understand that your chances of returning to school and achieving success are much greater today. With the support services now available on college campuses, many students with learning problems are completing their college degrees—even medical, law, and graduate degrees.

ADHD–LD Success Stories

Many adults with ADHD and LD have been able to achieve career success. With the recognition and support that are developing today, the chance of success for someone with ADHD and LD is even greater. Let's take a look at several successful adults who have both attention and learning difficulties.

First, a success story from the bad old days, before learning disorders were understood or accommodations made to them.

Warren is a college graduate and a successful computer specialist in his forties. He has ADHD and learning disorders. Although highly intelligent in things mechanical and mathematical, he has tremendous difficulty with written expression and with spelling. Warren attended college in the years before there were services for those with learning disorders on the college level.

During high school, Warren had shown tremendous ability and interest in certain activities. For example, he was a gifted amateur photographer and greatly enjoyed working behind the scenes on school plays. His handwriting, however, was almost illegible, and he struggled tremendously with written assignments.

Warren entered a state college, where he had the good fortune of meeting a professor who was to become his saving grace. This man, recognizing a real gift in Warren for things logical and systematic, became his mentor, serving as a source

(story continued)
of emotional support and as an educational advocate. He steered Warren toward professors who required minimal writing and on occasion convinced some of them to reexamine Warren verbally when he failed a written exam. By taking most of his courses in areas with minimal writing requirements and with the support and intervention of this wonderful man, who became a lifelong mentor, Warren was able to graduate from college and achieve tremendous success in the field of computer science.

Warren received no help to improve his writing difficulties. However, he did receive accommodations—inasmuch as he was able to avoid classes with written requirements and was on occasion permitted to take exams orally. Moreover, he had a mentor who encouraged and believed in him. Finally, he understood his gifts at an early age and chose a field that minimized his disorders and maximized his strengths.

Now let's take a look at a woman who had struggled all her life with learning disorders and had assumed she was "stupid."

Frances was a middle-aged woman who had barely graduated from a Southern finishing school many years ago. She always had difficulties in school, but her ADHD and LD were not diagnosed until she was in her fifties. After many years as a housewife and mother, Frances entered the job market following a divorce, terrified that her age-old problems with learning would emerge again. As a young woman, she had escaped into marriage and motherhood, and until her divorce, she had avoided new learning situations as much as possible.

As she began to understand her learning disorders, Frances began a healing process. While she had always labeled

(story continued)
herself stupid, she learned through testing that she had an above-average IQ. Her academic difficulties had been due to memory and oral comprehension problems. In other words, it was difficult for Frances to understand new information when it was presented to her orally (as most new information is!), and she had great difficulty recalling what she had heard.

Armed with this new understanding and with the ongoing help of a tutor, Frances made major changes in her life. Through her tutor, she learned memory-improvement techniques. To compensate for her memory problems, she requested written communication at work. She learned the technique of reviewing information in writing to enhance and reinforce oral information, and she learned to habitually take notes whenever information was presented to her orally.

After several months with her tutor, learning ways to remediate and compensate, Frances was a different person on the job—interested, inquisitive, and motivated. She no longer felt that her "stupidity" would soon be discovered, and she had lost much of her fear of learning new information.

Our third success story is about a college graduate who was diagnosed with ADHD in middle age following her teenage daughter's ADHD diagnosis. This is the only one of the three success stories presented in this chapter that involves a person who took advantage of the new services available on the college level.

Joanne sought an evaluation for ADHD when she recognized many of the same behavior patterns in herself that she saw in her daughter, who had recently been diagnosed with ADHD. During the course of her evaluation, it became clear that learning

(story continued)
difficulties, in addition to ADHD, had interfered with Joanne's academic functioning during her high school and college years.

Although a college graduate, Joanne had a spotty employment record and felt she had been a failure on many of her jobs. Testing for learning disorders showed that Joanne had two major areas of difficulty—memory and written language. Like many others with an LD–ADHD success story, Joanne learned that her IQ was above average. Her ability to comprehend complex ideas was high, but her ability to memorize and recall detailed information was much lower. Although she had good verbal expressive skills, Joanne had tremendous difficulty organizing her thoughts and putting them into writing.

As a result of her testing, Joanne developed the courage to return to school, and with the help of ADHD–LD career counseling, she selected the field of social work, where she could take advantage of her gifts of oral expression and could emphasize her strong capacity to understand and work with abstract concepts.

To aid her writing difficulty, Joanne began working regularly with a writing tutor, even before her classes in social work began. Although writing always presented a challenge for her, after working with a tutor for a year Joanne earned As consistently on all her graduate school papers, was enthusiastic about her future career as a social worker, and no longer considered herself "not very smart."

If You Think You Might Have a Learning Disorder

Too many adults with ADHD become over focused on their ADHD and ignore other issues that may be getting in their way. Don't cheat yourself by ignoring possible learning disorders. If you checked off a number of items on the ADHD Workplace Questionnaire relating to cognitive difficulties, you should seek an evaluation from a qualified expert. If the professional who is treating your ADHD is not well versed in LD diagnosis and treatment, you may need to work with an LD expert as well. And don't let a misinformed professional tell you that an assessment is no longer relevant because you are past your school days. Being diagnosed and receiving treatment for a learning disorder is the first crucial step toward taking charge of learning challenges that may be limiting your success on the job.

Note

1 Learning Disabilities Association of America (LDA), www.ldaamerica.org.

This chapter focuses on aspects of ADHD that may have a positive influence on your performance at work. Many traits can be either positive or negative depending upon the context in which you are working.

7

Putting the Positive Side of ADHD to Work

The chances are you are reading this book because ADHD has led to difficulties for you at work. It is extremely important, however, not to lose track of the potentially positive side of ADHD. There are many adults with ADHD who have been enormously successful in life despite their ADHD—even, in many respects, because of their ADHD. That's right, *because of it*! There is an upside to ADHD for many people. As is true for the downside of ADHD, people differ with respect to the positive ADHD traits they possess. It's important that you make a realistic assessment of yourself. If you can recognize your positive ADHD traits and learn how to take advantage of them, you can make the best choices about where to put those positive traits to work.

The Positive Side of ADHD

Just what are the positive aspects of ADHD? Most of what has been written about ADHD emphasizes areas of *dys*function. If you travel within the community of ADHD adults, however, you will encounter a different story. The following page shows a list of positive traits associated with ADHD adults, a list that was developed by an adult ADHD support group.

The "Up" Side of ADHD	
Creative	Good in a crisis
Resilient	Able to hyperfocus on projects
Energetic	Love a challenge
Enthusiastic	Love to interact with people
Determined	Good at communicating
Can think "on their feet"	Seek variety and stimulation

How many of these traits do you have? Studying this list may be a starting point for you in putting your ADHD to work for you!

Redefining Negative ADHD Traits

The list was developed expressly to emphasize the positive side of ADHD. But even some aspects of ADHD that are generally considered problematic can be positive attributes in the right situation. Whether a trait is an asset or a liability is often determined by the environment in which the individual is living and working.

Distractible or Superobservant?

Another way to describe those who are distractible is to say that they are highly observant. Their attention is attracted by the most minute change in the environment. Lara Honos-Webb, in her book *The Gift of Adult ADD*,[1] talks about how many of the very traits that are viewed by some as problematic can become gifts that lead to success in your career. One woman with ADHD used her visual distractibility to great advantage in the restaurant she owned and managed with her husband. Her energy and hypervigilance led her to automatically notice the smallest detail and kept her fine-dining restaurant running smoothly.

Internal Distractions or Rich Imagination?

Many individuals with ADHD enjoy a rich imagination. They make rapid and unique associations between different facts and fields. Often such individuals find that their best ideas come to them when they are working on something else entirely. If you can learn to harness your creativity by recording and later returning to your ideas, you have turned this "deficit" into a marvelous strength. One renowned scientist who was diagnosed with ADHD reported that this rapid flow of ideas and associations was his greatest asset as a scientist.

Hyperfocusing or Enormous Capacity to Concentrate?

Many successful people take great advantage of their tendency to hyperfocus. People from any field that calls upon concentrated, creative thought—writers, musicians, computer experts, designers, engineers, scientists—are at an enormous advantage if they are able to hyperfocus for long hours while working.

Impulsive or Capable of Quick Responses?

Impulsive people are quick reactors. Often they are more effective than reflective people in situations that call for quick responses. For example, one ADHD adult has developed a highly successful career in

California as a freelance television journalist. He has capitalized on his quick, impulsive style. He listens to the radio and to the police radio throughout the day. He has a history of being the first one on the spot with the best film footage of a newsworthy event. Impulsive people are more likely to seize the moment, take the chance, make the sale, grab the opportunity.

Hyperactivity or High Energy Level?

Hyperactivity and restlessness can also be seen as having high energy—a tremendously positive trait if you can find appropriate outlets for it. Many high-energy people become entrepreneurs, a lifestyle that allows them to take full advantage of their high energy level and that gives them the freedom to minimize activities that are sedentary.

Inattention to Detail or Capacity to See the Big Picture?

"Big picture" people can make tremendous contributions to an organization. They often have vision and are highly motivated to come up with new programs and procedures. Whether you are in a large organization or are creating your own entrepreneurial enterprise, you can turn such traits to your advantage.

Easily Bored or Tremendous Capacity for Innovation?

So many people with ADHD are described as easily bored—as if that were a negative trait that they would be so much better off without! But intolerance of the mundane and routine can lead to enormous creativity and innovation.

An ADHD Perspective on the Rest of the World

One of the most important messages in Thorn Hartmann's book *The Edison Gene*[2] is how the negative definition of ADHD can be turned on its head. Hartmann describes adults with ADHD as "hunters" and non–ADHD adults as "farmers." He emphasizes the positive aspects of these hunters and underlines their tremendous potential and actual contributions to our society.

Because ADHD has been so negatively defined by the farmers of our society, as an exercise in fair play, let's describe the farmer from the perspective of hunters. We might, for example, say that the farmer suffers from attention excess disorder, whose symptoms are as follows:

"Attention Excess Disorder"
Prefers following established routines
Moderate to low energy level
Low tolerance for change or ambiguity
Low tolerance for risk
Limited capacity to respond quickly in crisis situations
Slow, laborious decision making
Limited capacity to find novel solutions
Tends to think in a linear fashion
Processes and interprets incoming stimuli slowly

Any set of patterns and tendencies can be described in a biased and negative way. Obviously, there are advantages and disadvantages to being either a hunter with attention deficit disorder or a farmer with attention excess disorder. The important message for adults with ADHD is not to buy into the farmer's view of ADHD. People, with or without ADHD, have both strengths and weaknesses. The important issue is to understand those positives and negatives and to place yourself where your talents and abilities are most likely to thrive.

Going Overboard on the Positive ADHD Perspective

Both Lara Honos-Webb and Thorn Hartmann place tremendous emphasis on the positive side of ADHD. In fact, the positive emphasis of both writers has stirred debate in the ADHD community. Some feel that Hartmann and Honos-Webb have almost ignored the serious struggles of adults with ADHD by too strongly emphasizing the positive. They fear that ADHD has been trivialized and that efforts to better understand this disorder and to develop improved treatment approaches for it will not receive the time, attention, and badly needed research dollars it deserves.

Both authors describe adults with ADHD who are not severely affected and who have the capacity to succeed in spite of (and even because of) ADHD traits. Hartmann clearly states that his intention is to write about and for those adults with ADHD who have above-average intelligence and ability. He leaves to other writers the task of addressing the needs of the ADHD population that has more significant struggles.

Keep a Balanced View

The important issue for you, as an adult with ADHD, is to recognize that there are positive aspects to ADHD. By focusing only on the problem side of ADHD, you are less likely to appreciate your abilities. With a balanced view of yourself, you are better prepared to make good career choices.

Successful People with ADHD

There is a growing list of well-known adults who have been diagnosed with ADHD. Quite a number of famous people have been nominated as ADHD successes on the basis of their known traits and behaviors.[3] Among them are John Kennedy, Thomas Edison, Nelson Rockefeller, Bill Clinton, Winston Churchill, Benjamin Franklin, and Robin Williams.

The worlds of politics, comedy, music, athletics, sales, television, and entrepreneurial enterprises are likely places to look for successful ADHD adults. Does this mean you should try to head in those directions? Not necessarily. We know about them because they entered fields in which fame is part of the package for successful politicians and entertainers. There are many more that have entered into entrepreneurial endeavors and have found tremendous success but not fame. And there are those that work in media-related activities, helping build the fame of entertainers and politicians, who also have ADHD. For example, among those cameramen that have filmed me for interviews over the years, most of them have confided in me following the interview that they also have ADHD!

Since most of us aren't headed for fame, it is probably more helpful to focus on more ordinary ADHD adults who have become successful. These are not adults who have world-class looks, musical ability, or athletic skills but, rather, people who, by good fortune or good judgment, put themselves in circumstances that have allowed them to soar. Let's look at people of different ages and educational and social backgrounds who have succeeded because of their positive ADHD traits. In each of these stories, I have used pseudonyms in order to protect the privacy of the individuals involved. The circumstances of their lives have been altered only in ways to protect their privacy, but the important and essential facts of their stories are true and current. First, let's take a look at Chris, now in his late twenties. Chris was the out-of-wedlock child of a teenage mother.

From the outset, Chris was clearly hyperactive. In addition to his unstoppable energy, Chris, a handsome boy, was very talkative and curious. When he entered school, he showed no patience for the passive activities of reading and writing. Luckily for Chris, his family did not turn Chris's dislike of school into a huge battle.

Chris's mother and stepfather owned and managed a small family business. After school each day, Chris walked to his parents' store. He was gradually put to work in the store and thus learned to function in the business world as naturally as he had learned to talk.

Chris loved automobiles and talked of little else. At sixteen, he was hired by an automobile agency. At eighteen, Chris became the youngest car salesman ever at the dealership. His ready smile, his energy, and his sociability carried him far. By the age of thirty, this ADHD high school graduate owned his own home, drove an expensive company car, and earned more than $100,000 per year. He was brimming with enthusiasm and self-confidence.

John was the son of a highly regarded businessman. He grew up in the suburbs of Washington, D.C., attending one of the competitive, suburban high schools from which many students go on to top colleges and universities. John, to the embarrassment of his parents, was a poor student. Although bright, he showed no motivation in high school.

Prompted by depression, frustration, and chronic conflicts with his parents, John drifted into frequent marijuana use and fairly heavy drinking in his late adolescence. He entered the local community college, but his lethargy and low motivation continued. Meanwhile, he developed an interest in computers and electronics. He dropped out of community college to seek training in a local computer school to become a computer technician.

(story continued)

You might ask yourself at this point, "How is this a success story?" John's story begins differently from Chris's largely because of the conflict John had with his parents. In John's case there was a tremendous gap between his natural inclinations and his parents' expectations.

After John completed his nine-month course in computer programming, he found an entry-level job as a computer technician. Several years later, he married. With the support of a non–ADHD wife and with the responsibilities of marriage, John's attitude toward education began to change. He slowly began to take college courses at night. This time, with a focus and with motivation, he set his sights on a degree in computer science.

By his mid-thirties, John had received several promotions at work. In his early forties, he earned a master's degree in business administration. By his mid-forties, John held a very responsible position in the computer science industry. At this point, I lost track of John. He was doing well and had no need for my services. But there's an even better ending to his story. He contacted me about ten years later to tell me he had founded his own company, a company that focused on two things he loved—computers and fast cars—and had developed a computerized fuel-injection system that was now being used by top race car drivers!

What factors had led to John's eventual success?

- He had wisely decided to pursue a career path that greatly interested him and for which he showed a natural talent.
- He was helped tremendously by the support and structure provided by his non–ADHD spouse, who believed in him and encouraged him to pursue his interests.

- He was able to motivate and discipline himself to continue his education because he selected courses of study that had a direct and practical relationship to his work.
- He persisted. John's education was not completed until age forty-five. He never gave up.

It is critical that adults with ADHD not measure themselves by the yardstick of "normality." As we saw with John, many adults who become successful despite ADHD do so later than their peers and via a more nontraditional path.

Mark sought help for his ADHD in his early thirties, when he feared losing his job as an accountant. He was the son of a successful accountant and had chosen that career after failing to earn a degree in engineering. Although he was highly intelligent and curious and had a lively imagination, Mark had never shown much discipline or motivation to succeed in school.

Although Mark was intelligent and likable, his habitual late arrival and indifferent work habits finally prompted his supervisor to give him a stern warning. Mark discussed his career problems with a friend, who suggested that his lifelong problems with self-discipline and motivation might be related to ADHD. Mark sought an evaluation, and his friend's suspicions were quickly confirmed. He embarked on a treatment program that included both medication and career-oriented counseling.

Mark's low motivation at work and at school were in great contrast to his intense interest in a wide range of hobbies. Now he began to explore, with his counselor, ways his work life could become more fun. Mark loved computers and was gregarious, with a gift for verbal expression. It had simply never occurred to him that these interests and abilities might be applied to his career in accounting.

(story continued)

He began to explore with his supervisor the possibility of transferring to a job in the firm that would take advantage of his computer expertise and his natural gift for teaching and explaining. The more convincingly he demonstrated his newfound motivation at work, the more willing his supervisor became to support him in new career directions.

Two years after Mark's initial diagnosis of ADHD, he was happily ensconced in a new position with his firm, training coworkers to use new software systems. He was excited about his work, which was a good match for his interests and abilities, and felt positive about his future in the firm.

What were the factors that led to Mark's career success?

- His high natural ability.
- Positive ADHD traits—curiosity, inventiveness, high energy level, and a gregarious, outgoing nature.
- He responded well to treatment for his ADHD.
- He was able to carve out a niche that was a very good match for his interests and abilities.

Karen's success was entirely self-made. She sought an evaluation in her late fifties after reading articles on ADHD. The story she told was of almost heroic proportions.

Karen was raised in a dysfunctional home. Her parents divorced when she was young. Her mother, not highly educated herself, had little time or energy to devote to her daughter. This timid, underweight little girl was sent to classes for underachievers, where she languished for years.

(story continued)

She was almost illiterate when she graduated from high school, but somewhere inside this young woman, there developed a steely determination to change her life. She set about to teach herself to read—and, amazingly, was successful in her effort. Despite a low-paying job and a failing marriage, she decided to go to college.

Karen's one stroke of luck was to land a job as a secretary for a government agency that paid her tuition as a fringe benefit. Her self-discipline and determination were evident on the job, and she was gradually promoted to higher and higher positions.

When Karen finally sought an ADHD evaluation in her late fifties, she reported that she had successfully raised her two children, had finally earned her college degree, was an active union representative, and had been taking courses in law school for the past several years. Her hope was that, with the benefit of treatment for her difficulties in concentration, she could take a leave of absence from her job, go to school full time, and succeed in her goal of becoming a labor lawyer. All this from a woman who was nearly illiterate and almost without a family when she graduated from high school.

The keys to Karen's success are more difficult to pinpoint, but they certainly include:

- Determination
- Perseverance
- Encouragement from professors
- Opportunity (through a tuition-reimbursement program at work)

Karen's story is inspiring as an example of how strong motivation can overcome enormous odds.

As you can see from these stories, success in life with ADHD can be reached through a variety of channels. All these people reached success by finding a type of work for which they were well suited and in which they were highly interested. Furthermore, in spite of the academic difficulties related to their ADHD they each experienced, they all possessed some positive ADHD characteristics as well, which contributed to their success. They learned how to make ADHD work for them rather than against them!

Notes

1 Honos-Webb, Lara. (2008). *The Gift of Adult ADD: How to Transform Your Challenges and Build on Your Strengths.* Oakland, CA: New Harbinger Publications.

2 Hartman, Thom. (2010). *The Edison Gene: ADHD and the Gift of the Hunter Child.* Paris, ME: Park Street Press.

3 Hartmann, T. (2010). *ADHD Secrets of Success: Coaching Yourself to Fulfillment in the Business World.* New York: SelectBooks.

IN THIS CHAPTER

If you have completed the ADHD Workplace Questionnaire (located in the Appendix), you have identified areas of challenge that you experience in your job. In this chapter, you'll learn coping techniques for dealing with these problems to reduce the negative impact of ADHD at work.

8

Taking Charge of Your ADHD at Work

What can you do to reduce the negative impact of your ADHD at work? In this chapter, I present strategies to directly address a wide range of ADHD challenges. It's important to keep in mind that ADHD is not the same in all people. Some of the patterns described may apply to you, while others may not. Focus on those sections that correspond to your particular concerns.

Inattention/Distractibility

Problems with distractibility can be either external (distractions in the environment) or internal (distractions due to internal thoughts, reactions, or daydreams).

Environmental Distractions

Our mental energy is drained by distractions and frequent interruptions. Working in an environment in which distractions and interruptions are frequent can significantly detract from your ability to be efficient and productive. Here are some suggestions for managing environmental distractions.

Strategies to Reduce Interruptions

- Shift your work hours to either come in early or stay late in order to increase interruption-free time at the office.
- Request to work from home part of the time.
- Request a private office, if available.
- Request to shift your work space to a less trafficked area.
- Close your office door (if you are fortunate enough to have one).

Strategies to Reduce Distracting Sounds

- Use headphones to help screen out distracting sounds.
- Use a fan or white-noise machine to muffle sounds.
- Use conference rooms or other available space when working on tasks that require particular concentration.
- Request sound-absorbing portable office partitions.
- Request an officemate whose work habits are less distracting.
- Use foam earplugs.

Strategies to Reduce Visual Distractions

- Turn your desk so it doesn't face the door.
- Don't set up your e-mail so that you are notified whenever a new message arrives.
- Work on a clear, uncluttered desk. Move all documents you're not working on to a different surface, such as a credenza behind you, or to the side.

- Turn off your Internet connectivity so the Internet is less accessible to you.

Internal Distractions

Many ADHD adults struggle as much, if not more, with internal as with external distractions.

- **"Ah ha!" Distractions**—Creative ideas that suddenly occur to you and take you off task can be managed by writing your ideas down before you return to your current task. By managing your "ah ha's," you can make them real assets rather than distractions from current work.
- **"Oh no!" Distractions**—The sudden intrusive memory of a forgotten task. Your solution can be found in learning to effectively use a day-planning system to record tasks, phone calls, meetings, and so on so you are less likely to forget. The key is to note the forgotten task and then get back to the task at hand.
- **"Ho hum" Distractions**—Work-avoidant daydreams. Your solution will come in finding ways to make your work more interesting or in seeking more interesting work elsewhere. Chronic daydreamers are often stuck in a poor job match.
- **"Getting lost in the weeds" Distractions**—Some individuals with ADHD struggle greatly with a tendency to go into more detail than is required for the job. It may help to set an alarm to go off every 20 minutes as a reminder to check that tendency and get on with the task.

Hyperfocusing

Hyperfocusing is a state of intense focus. When someone hyperfocuses, he or she tends to lose track of time and may spend far more time than he or she had allocated on a given task. While hyperfocus can lead to tremendous productivity, it can also derail your daily schedule.

Some adults with ADHD report that they become so oblivious when working that they miss meetings and lunch appointments and otherwise lose all track of time. Less-engaging aspects of your job tend to go entirely ignored as you hyperfocus on what fascinates you. Here are some coping techniques:

- Look for a compatible work environment in which total immersion and lack of social interaction are acceptable.
- Learn to cue yourself. This might mean setting an alarm or perhaps asking a coworker to tap on your shoulder or your door as he or she leaves for a meeting or lunch.
- Plan your periods of hyperfocusing so that they don't interfere with scheduled commitments.
- Get the boring stuff out of the way, then hyperfocus to your heart's content.

Impulsivity

Extreme impulsivity can be very destructive in the workplace, not to mention all other aspects of life. Highly impulsive individuals are sometimes prone to make major life decisions without much thought of the consequences. They may repeatedly leave jobs on impulse, never staying long enough to find solutions or compromises; they commit to projects or tasks without considering whether they have the time or resources. Impulsivity can lead to great inefficiency. Jumping into a project without forethought or planning leads to blunders, ineffectiveness, and disorganization. Here are some coping techniques to manage impulsivity.

Impulsive Job Hopping

Learn to better understand your needs. Analyze whether a job is suitable for you *before* accepting it. If you need work immediately and don't have time for careful job matching, consider temping while you work to better understand your needs and talents. If you are more thoughtful in accepting your next job, you will be less likely to quit impulsively.

Making Impulsive Commitments

Rather than giving an automatic "yes" when someone suggests a new idea or project, learn a catchphrase such as "I'd like to, but let me take a look at my calendar." This phrase can act as a set of brakes for you. With a little time for reflection, you'll be able to make sounder decisions.

Jumping in without a Plan

This lack of planning can be a very inefficient way of doing things and is discussed more fully in the section titled "Problems with Organization" later in this chapter.

Impulsively Promising More Than You Can Deliver

Many individuals with ADHD greatly underestimate how long tasks will take them. In order to please their boss or coworkers, they may tend to make promises they then can't keep. Instead, try to get into the habit of under-promising and over-delivering! Whatever time you think a task will take, double it and tell your colleagues you'll be able to fulfill their request in double whatever time you think it will take. Then get down to work and surprise everyone by turning it in ahead of time.

General Impulsivity

In general, the rule is to slow down and take time to consider. If you have already acted impulsively—by making a commitment or decision that you haven't thought through—go back and "undo" it quickly. It's much easier to change your commitment without serious consequence to your coworkers if you do it right away, before others have moved ahead on a project counting on your participation. Tell them you remain very interested in the project (if this is the case), but after consulting your calendar and reflecting realistically, you realize you won't be able to manage the new project on top of those you're already committed to.

Impulsive Reactions to Others

Interpersonal impulsivity is a major concern for some people with ADHD. Interpersonal impulsivity may take the form of frequently interrupting others or overreacting to others when upset or frustrated. This is such an important issue that I've devoted a whole chapter to the effect of ADHD on relationships in the workplace (see Chapter 9).

Hyperactivity

The great majority of jobs today are sedentary, which poses a very difficult challenge if you are an adult with hyperactive tendencies. Even though you may be much less hyperactive than you were as a child or teen, many adults with ADHD continue to feel restless and in need of movement. Their tapping, walking, and wandering can easily be misinterpreted as boredom, disinterest, or low motivation. Additionally, when hyperactive people do things at a quick pace, they sometimes frustrate or fluster coworkers who prefer to work at a more measured pace. Here are some things you can do at work to cope with restlessness and hyperactivity:

- "Fidget" intentionally by taking notes during meetings. This not only will provide you with an activity but will also impress your coworkers that you are paying attention. Writing what you hear will also will enhance your concentration and memory.
- Engage in productive activities that require movement—pick up the mail, walk to the copy machine, get a cup of coffee, walk to your colleague's office rather than calling him or her on the phone—when you need a break from sedentary activity.

- Bring your lunch. This will allow you time to exercise during your lunch break.
- If you have a private office, take brief exercise breaks every hour or two.
- Build more movement and activity into your life outside work; for example, park farther away from the office and walk to work from there.
- Do aerobic exercise for at least one half hour before or after work.
- Intentionally choose work that routinely allows movement; work in sales, construction, repair, servicing, law enforcement, photo journalism, training, teaching, hospitality, or fire protection.
- Consider two part-time jobs rather than one full-time job to increase movement and variety.

Need for Stimulation (Intolerance of Routine)

Many jobs entail repetitive, uninteresting work, some more than others. Often, adults with ADHD grow bored by detailed paperwork and record-keeping tasks that inevitably follow the creative, exciting start-up phase of projects. Here are some suggestions to deal with them:

- If you have the opportunity, team up with a coworker whose strengths are in your areas of weakness (look for a partner who is good at details and day-to-day management).
- If you do not have this luxury, look for assistance or training to improve your skills in organization.
- If possible, choose work that allows a high degree of variety and change.
- Look for work that calls for a minimum of record-keeping and paperwork.
- If you work for yourself, hire someone to manage the details and maintain your records.

Memory Difficulties

Many ADHD adults exhibit poor short-term memory; they absentmindedly misplace items, lock their keys in their car, or forget to carry through on verbal requests from others. Frequent forgetting at work can be misperceived as irresponsibility or poor motivation. The following list shows practical approaches that some adults with ADHD have found helpful.

Tips for Combating Poor Short-Term Memory

1. Carry a day planner or smartphone with you at *all* times to record notes.
2. Avoid situations in which you receive information without the opportunity to write it down.
3. Don't write notes on scraps of paper—only in your day planner.
4. Always take notes during meetings.
5. Ask coworkers to e-mail or fax rather than call—this provides a written record.
6. Avoid interruptions whenever possible. Close your door; send calls to voicemail.
7. Use a voice recorder.
8. Develop a beeper or reminder system on your watch or computer to cue you regarding scheduled tasks or events.
9. Use visual prompts like sticky notes. Place reminder objects where you'll see them: by the front door, in the front seat of your car.
10. Visualize to pre-rehearse a sequence of things you need to do.
11. Develop routines. They place less demand on your memory.

Time Management

Running Late

"Running late" is an almost classic ADHD pattern. There are several coping techniques:

- Plan to arrive early to allow for unforeseen events. If none occur, your early arrival will allow time to plan, focus, take notes, or reread memos or e-mails, allowing you to be well prepared and focused for the scheduled event.
- Don't give in to the "just-one-more-thing-itis." If you think of one more thing to do as you prepare to leave, write down your thought in your day planner and act on it later.
- Be on the lookout for impulses that occur on the way to do something else. One man with ADHD found that even after he had mastered leaving for work early, he still on occasion arrived at the office late because he gave in to impulses along the way.
- Build in "getting ready" time. For some adults with ADHD, the "it's time to go" cue often becomes the "it's time to get ready" cue. Only then do they ask themselves such questions as "What do I need to take with me?" or "What is the phone number in case I get lost?" These questions are important, but they should be asked—and answered—well before it's time to walk out the door.

Overcommitment

Another classic ADHD time-management problem is overcommitment, that is, deciding to do things you really don't have time to do and then attempting to squeeze them in anyway. Whether this kind of overcommitment occurs on a large scale at work or on a small scale with friends or family, it can wreak havoc with your ability to conduct life in any kind of orderly fashion. Here are a couple techniques to help you cope with overcommitment:

- Make it a habit to say "Let me check my calendar" before accepting a new commitment.
- Try to catch yourself before giving in to an impulse to squeeze something into your busy schedule. Finish the already-scheduled things first. Then, if you have time, you can add other things to your list.
- If you add a commitment, then you must subtract a previous commitment. Remember, your time is not infinitely expandable.

Procrastination

Procrastination is a major time-management problem for many people with ADHD, especially for tasks that are either difficult or uninteresting. Here are some coping techniques for managing a tendency to procrastinate:

- Look for jobs in which there is a minimum of tedious paperwork—paperwork is the number-one procrastination item.
- Look for jobs in which there are few long-term projects requiring a large report at the end. Reports are another item that typically poses major problems for ADHD procrastinators.
- Commit yourself to a deadline and declare it to colleagues or to your supervisor. Making a promise to others often helps people overcome their own resistance.
- Set up a weekly progress report with your boss in which you make a detailed plan for each week and then report on task completion in the next week's progress report.

Paperwork Problems at Work

Paperwork is typically problematic for adults with ADHD. Problems can range from relatively minor ones (e.g., turning in your expense record or time sheet late) to major ones, such as losing important material or not completing paperwork critical to the functioning of your organization.

Why do these problems happen? A number of ADHD traits come together to create the paperwork pile: impatience with detail, a tendency to put off doing boring, unessential things, and a tendency to toss papers onto a "get around to it" pile. To cope with this problem, you can try the following:

- Look for work that has a minimum of paperwork.
- Look for ways to streamline your job to reduce paperwork.
- Find ways to reward yourself for completing unavoidable paperwork.
- Develop a more streamlined filing system to make your filing chores easier and less tedious.
- Do tedious tasks regularly, in small bits—do not let the filing or correspondence pile up and become overwhelming.
- Do paperwork at a time of day during which you are least tired. Some have found that doing paperwork first thing in the morning is more successful than putting it off until the end of the day, when you're likely to feel tired and ready to stop for the day.

Problems with Organization

Many ADHD adults have a tendency to jump into tasks and figure them out as they go. This approach can work for some relatively simple tasks but becomes less desirable when a task is more complicated. The impromptu approach is most likely to fail when the project is complex or must be coordinated with the work of others. Here are some tips to consider if you have problems with organization:

- Start at the end and work backward. Mark on a calendar when your project is due and then work backward, indicating on the calendar the various dates by which earlier stages must be completed. This approach often results in a more realistic time line.
- Make it visual. For many adults with ADHD, "out of sight is out of mind." Make a large chart of time lines for all your projects, and place it on the wall of your cubicle or office so you can readily check what needs to be done when.
- Divide projects into bite-sized tasks. Reward yourself for the completion of each task.
- Prioritize and plan with a coworker or supervisor.

Difficulty with Long-Term Follow-Through

Some behavior patterns that may appear to be procrastination are actually a product of distractibility and poor organization. An ADHD adult may have a host of projects that have been left undone because his or her flow of ideas have led him or her farther and farther away from his or her original task. He or she may be simply caught up in the project of the moment and may have little or none of the negative, avoidant pattern present in procrastination. Such ADHD adults are often enthusiastic, energetic initiators who, being drawn from one interesting idea or impulse to the next, are simply ineffective in task completion. If this description fits you, consider these tips:

- Use a day-planning system religiously.
- Take a course in time management and organization.

- Work with a partner or group that can help keep you on task.
- Establish a pattern of daily or weekly reporting to your supervisor to help keep you focused.
- Each evening or first thing in the morning, spend ten minutes deciding on "must-do" priorities for the day rather than just diving in and seeing where your impulses take you.

Difficulty Coordinating Simultaneous Tasks

Many bright, capable ADHD adults encounter severe performance problems at work when they are promoted to managerial positions in which they are expected to coordinate multiple projects and people. Jobs that require ADHD adults to oversee many people involved in several different projects may overtax their organizational capacity. They may encounter enormous difficulty monitoring both their own progress and the progress of the rest of a team involved in a complex, long-term project.

ADHD adults may frequently have the feeling they have been frantically busy all day but have accomplished little. In fact, their disorganization and forgetfulness may have created crises to which they then had to respond, further distracting them from attending to the most important aspects of their complex job. If you have difficulty coordinating several tasks at once, consider the following suggestions:

- Be realistic in assessing your managerial abilities. No matter how tempting a managerial position may seem initially, it may in the end bring more frustration than satisfaction.
- Try shifting the responsibility to your supervisees to check in with you rather than waiting for you to check up on them.
- Divide your day: Begin with supervisory tasks and then move to your own work. If you begin your own work first, you may

find that you have hyperfocused, overlooking your supervisory responsibilities.

- Carefully protect yourself from constant interruptions by those whom you supervise. Set aside times when you are available.

Conclusion

In this chapter, I have tried to deal in a limited space with a wide range of job performance difficulties often experienced by individuals with ADHD. The suggestions here are by no means exhaustive. Memory, time management, procrastination, planning, and organizational skills are all complex issues. Entire books have been devoted to each of them. The suggestions here are meant as a starting point for you. In order to succeed in really changing some of these troubling work patterns, you will need to devote extended time; moreover, you are likely to need the assistance of a tutor, counselor, or coach. Here are a few general suggestions for you:

- Don't try to tackle everything at once. Successes tend to build, one on top of the other. For example, better time management on your part will enhance your later efforts toward better organization and planning.
- Build habits. Pick a crucial area, identify some practical approaches, and then keep at it until you have developed a new habit.
- Use others to keep you focused. A coach or counselor may be useful to help you figure out where things are going wrong and to suggest a different approach.
- Be realistic. Some people with ADHD, determined to master their difficulties, create their own downfall by sticking with a job for which they are poorly suited. Your efforts will be much better spent if you choose a job wisely, one that calls upon your strengths, and then work on habit building in an ADHD–friendly environment.

Many adults with ADHD find that they are most effective in beginning to implement some of these approaches when they work regularly with a therapist and/or an ADHD coach who helps them prioritize, keep focused, and problem solve when things go wrong.

The reader may want to use my book *ADD–Friendly Ways to Organize Your Life* as a companion to this book. *ADD–Friendly Ways* focuses entirely on planning and organizing strategies that can be implemented in all aspects of daily life, including the workplace. Using this book while working with a coach can prove very beneficial. Remember, don't try to do too many things at once, and don't try to do it all alone. Habits take time to build! If you are patient with yourself, you may be very pleased to recognize how much better organized and efficient you are a year or so from now.

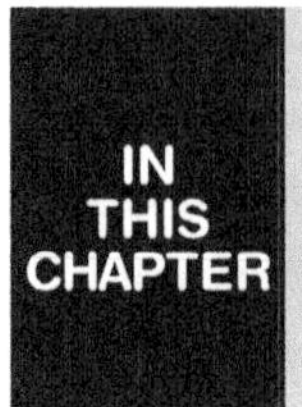

Your relationships with others at work are key to job satisfaction and good work performance. In this chapter, people and communication patterns sometimes found in adults with ADHD are discussed, and suggestions are offered for ways to improve your people interactions at work.

9

Building Positive Relationships at Work

An essential part of top job performance depends on your ability to work well with others. Sadly, too many individuals with ADHD have lost their jobs not because they could not do the job but because they could not work comfortably and collaboratively with others. An adult with ADHD might feel resentful about a colleague being promoted ahead of him or her, having no awareness that the promotion resulted from both competence and positive working relationships, particularly with the boss. The ADHD coworker might say angrily, "I could work circles around her! She just got in cozy with the boss," never realizing that his or her own blunt or argumentative approach was the culprit that repeatedly prevented him or her from being promoted. Sheer competence is a big plus, but it's rarely enough to do well at work.

In their book *When Smart People Fail,* Carole Hyatt and Linda Gottlieb describe their investigation of career failures among a group of smart, talented people in a broad range of professions.[1] They concluded that the most critical factor, by far, in career failure is related to interpersonal problems. No matter how talented and capable you may be, you cannot afford to ignore the importance of learning how to cooperate with others, to read social cues, to work as a team member, and to remain aware of how your attitudes and habits affect those you work with.

People skills can be even more critical when you have ADHD. By paying attention to your effect on others, by cooperating with them, and by showing consideration and tolerance of differences, you can build up goodwill, like credit in the bank, that you can later draw on if your ADHD inadvertently causes problems for others. If your coworkers know you, feel close to you, like you, and trust you, then you have a lot more leeway to make mistakes—and opportunity to learn from those mistakes. If you make sure your positives outweigh the negatives, some of your ADHD–related errors will be tolerated or overlooked.

Build credits in your "goodwill account" at work through positive work relations to prevent ADHD slip-ups from overdrawing your account.

Tuning in to How You Affect Others at Work

Most of the interpersonal difficulties created by adults with ADHD are completely unintentional and are often created even without their awareness. In fact, awareness of behavior patterns that may cause interpersonal difficulties is the first and most crucial step toward reducing those patterns. In this chapter, we'll look at some of the most common ways someone with ADHD might unintentionally step on others' toes at work.

After reading this chapter, if you recognize some of these patterns in yourself, it may be useful for you to work with an ADHD career counselor or ADHD psychotherapist on making changes. Additionally, if you have a trusted coworker who can give you a friendly hint when you are overstepping boundaries at work, you can make a correction more quickly. A quick, sincere apology followed by genuine efforts to change a problem behavior will go a long way toward smoothing ruffled feathers.

Good People Skills at Work

In any discussion of people skills in the workplace, a good place to start is with the basics—the nuts and bolts of good manners and good people skills. The workplace is a community of individuals engaged in interconnected, cooperative efforts who spend the majority of their waking hours together. Paying attention to the basics of good manners and good people skills in that community is essential.

Why Are Good People Skills More Challenging for Many Adults with ADHD?

People skills are more challenging for many individuals with ADHD because good people skills require paying close attention to complex group interactions. They involve ongoing monitoring of your effect on others while you go about your work. For adults with ADHD, this dual focus is often difficult to maintain. They may become so intent on the point they are making in a verbal discussion that they are unaware that they have become argumentative rather than persuasive. They may be so focused on "being right" that they don't listen, much less acknowledge, that others have valuable input to offer. They may become so engrossed in their work that they lose track of time and forget, for example, that they have promised to phone a colleague. They may be completely unaware that their tapping, fidgeting, or chair tipping is annoying to those around them. They may be so focused on the meeting agenda that they completely neglect the "small talk" that creates the social glue in an organization. Intense, argumentative, lost in your own thoughts, always late, unaware of irritating others, poor listener, interrupt to make your own point? Do some of these describe you?

Just Say "Hi"

Those with ADHD may feel preoccupied and stressed and forget to do the basics of a friendly hello and acknowledgement of others. "She left without evening saying good-bye!" or "He can't even be bothered to say 'Good morning!'" are comments frequently heard from colleagues and staff about preoccupied ADHD coworkers. The basics of saying hello at the beginning of the workday and good-bye as you depart are basic ways you acknowledge those around you. While the omission is most likely unintentional, it can leave a lot of interpersonal damage in its wake. If this preoccupied pattern of not saying hello describes your own behavior, you'll be pleasantly surprised at how quickly you can turn these negative perceptions around. "I don't know what happened, but she's a lot more friendly these days," or "He seems to be in a better mood lately" are comments that will begin to emerge in response to your new rule:

**When You Arrive,
Say "Hi"; When You Leave,
Say "Good-Bye"**

Try this simple formula for a couple weeks and see what happens. I predict you'll see a lot more smiles coming your way.

Always Running Late?

No matter how hard you work or how brilliant your contribution, the negative impressions you make through lateness tend to endure. Chronic lateness suggests lack of discipline, lack of organization, lack of professionalism, and lack of regard for others. Routinely arriving late for meetings gives the impression that you consider your time more valuable than that of your coworkers.

Make your new motto "On time *all* the time."

Tips for Becoming an On-Time Person

- Take time management step by step. Good time management requires building a whole set of habits and can't be done overnight.
- Let your supervisor and coworkers know you take your time problems seriously and are working hard to change your habits.
- A good place to start is by arriving at work on time. Running late in the morning may be related to a number of things:
    - Getting to bed too late the night before (you may have sleep problems that need treatment)
    - Habitual "escapist" activities at night that make you tired the next day (computer games, television, detective books, and so on)
    - Not allowing enough time in the morning
    - Allowing distractions to get in the way in the morning
    - Never allowing extra time for traffic jams or other unforeseen events
- Try to arrive early for all events. Many people with ADHD hate to wait and therefore avoid being early. As a result, they are often late. Bring something to read or work on so that if you succeed in arriving early, you can use the time productively and won't feel impatient.
- Try to pinpoint patterns that lead to chronic lateness—for example:
    - Answering the phone when you're on your way out the door
    - Impulsively trying to do one more thing before you leave

Tips for Becoming an On-Time Person *(continued)*

- Getting involved in some activity—reading the paper, watching the news, engaging in conversation—and then losing track of the time

Putting Things Off Puts People Off!

Putting *things* off puts *people* off! While many ADHD adults are quite aware of their tendency to procrastinate and the problems it causes *them,* they may be less aware of the problems their procrastination causes for others. Procrastination patterns almost always have a negative impact on coworkers. Unless your projects are entirely independent (which is rarely the case), your procrastination is likely to create frustration and resentment among the members of your team. Often they cannot complete some portion of their own work until they have received yours.

One scientist caused such frustration among his fellow researchers by consistently completing his work late over the course of years that several members of his team went to great lengths to terminate their long-term relationship with him.

To combat this tendency, use the following strategies:

- Create a series of intermediate deadlines.
- Meet regularly with team members and set short-term goals; weekly goals, and even daily ones, can be very helpful in avoiding procrastination on large long-term projects.
- Identify the activities that are most likely to produce procrastination (these are often tasks that involve paperwork, such as writing summaries, reports, articles, or budgets) and try to organize the project so you have reduced responsibility for such tasks.
- Team up with someone who is less likely to procrastinate.
- Volunteer for activities that are immediate and therefore cannot be put off.

- Don't expect your procrastination to be tolerated. Apologize when it occurs and make genuine efforts to make amends.

Remember:

Putting *things* off
Puts *people* off.

Learn to Make a Good First Impression

Whether you are beginning a new job or simply starting a new work assignment with a team you are less familiar with, you have entered foreign territory. Until you have been on the job or a member of the team long enough to become an insider, it is important to recognize your newcomer status and behave accordingly. This means getting the lay of the land and understanding the politics of your new office environment before venturing to express your own opinions. This prolonged period of reticence can be difficult for some adults with ADHD. If you impulsively express your opinions or ask indiscreet questions you may unwittingly offend your coworkers, thereby making your acceptance by others in the new work environment more difficult. Here are some tips for newcomers:

- If you have ideas for changes or innovations, write them down. This will help you restrain yourself from expressing them, and they may prove valuable later.
- Look for someone who seems friendly and approachable. He or she may be able to introduce you to the interpersonal landscape of your new job.
- Engage in self-talk. Remind yourself repeatedly that you need to "stop, look, and listen" rather than barge in too soon.
- Talk less, listen more.

- Be a team player—volunteer when appropriate.
- Don't ask personal questions, but let others get to know you. The more open you are, the more you'll put others at ease.
- Don't make comments to new coworkers about others on the team.
- Don't jump in with both feet. Others may not like the splash you make!

**Before you jump in . . .
Count to 10.**

Are You a Space or Time Invader?

Many ADHD adults may unintentionally create in others a feeling of being invaded. Without awareness or intention, adults with ADHD are prone to interrupt conversations, borrow items (owing to their disorganization) and forget to return them, and spread their belongings around in a way that interferes with others. These tendencies are among the behaviors you should be super vigilant about, especially when you enter a new work environment. Consider the following solutions:

- Look for ways to confine your work and belongings to a circumscribed area.
- Make it a top priority to obtain needed items for yourself rather than continue to borrow from others.
- Always ask first—don't assume it's OK to use or borrow something.
- Always ask, "Have you got a minute?" when you enter someone's office or pass by their cubicle. Then keep it to a *minute*!
- Look *closely* for cues that your coworker is busy and wants to terminate the discussion. These cues might be looking away from you, turning back toward his or her desk, answering your questions very briefly, and not making remarks that would encourage more conversation.

Don't Make Your Boredom or Restlessness a Problem for Others

Due to a strong need for stimulation, some adults with ADHD can stir up extra work and extra trouble for coworkers. You may cause resentment as you leave the "dirty work" to others while you buzz off to create something new and interesting. To avoid such resentment:

- Don't just assume that someone else will pick up the pieces.
- Look for jobs in which your assigned work is stimulating so you are not continually looking for other tasks.
- Take on your fair share of the work that no one really cares to do!
- Be aware that others are not comfortable with your fast pace and need for stimulation.
- Be careful not to make more work for others as you seek new projects for yourself.

Paperwork

Paperwork problems are bound to have a negative impact on others, to some extent, in any job. No matter how well you do other aspects of your job, if you misfile, don't file, or can't find important documents, don't turn in time sheets routinely, and miss details, you will likely be seen as careless and as someone who can't really be depended on. Not only that, but others can't do their job until you turn in your paperwork. Here are some coping techniques:

- Keep your filing system as simple as possible so you will be more likely to file your papers. (One man with ADHD developed a filing system that consisted of a dozen boxes, clearly labeled and kept on shelves. Although it was not an elegant system, he found that he could at least get himself to toss papers in the appropriate box, whereas with a more traditional filing system, he tended to accumulate unfiled stacks of paper randomly situated throughout his office.)

- Filing systems that are easily accessible seem to work best. (Some ADHD adults work well with files in open carts, which can be seen and easily accessed.)
- Color-coded filing systems often work well for adults with ADHD. (Color code by broad category; for example, have one color for files you need to access frequently.)
- Whenever possible, avoid jobs that entail a great deal of filing and paperwork.
- If you file early in the day, the chore is more likely to get done.

Minimize paperwork to maximize success.

Have Trouble Organizing Your Tasks and Your Time?

An ADHD adult's problems with organization have the same sorts of impact on coworkers as his or her problems with time management and paperwork do. Your own disorganization spills over and affects the work of others. By working reactively rather than proactively, you are consciously or unconsciously depending on others to cue you as to what to do next.

- The single most important thing you can do to improve your organization is to use a dayplanner, take a training course on its use, and actively work toward the daily habit of using it to plan your day, week, and month.
- Adopt a "Do it now or write it down" rule.

- Look for ways to simplify your job—disorganization increases with complexity.
- Ask for assistance from your supervisor in setting work priorities.

Tuning Others Out

Some people with ADHD become so task focused that they overlook the tremendous importance of keeping the people wheels oiled at the office. This doesn't mean that you have to join in the gossip at the water cooler, but a friendly smile and a quick hello are essential to good working relationships.

If you unintentionally ignore others while hyperfocusing on your work, it will require an active effort on your part to change your pattern. Recognizing that people interaction in the workplace is essential is the first step (some people with ADHD tend to live in a cocoon of preoccupation, with little awareness of the reactions of others).

You cannot operate effectively in an organization if you are in a people vacuum. Through interaction with others, you develop networks, partnerships, and alliances and learn of important events and changes in the organization. Once you make a decision to change your people patterns, it will take conscious effort to develop new habits. Some approaches:

- Make a regular lunch date with coworkers.
- Arrive early at meetings in order to have an opportunity to talk.
- Make a conscious effort to greet people in the morning and to say good-bye before departing in the evening.

Oiling social wheels will keep your project running smoothly.

Distracting Others from Their Work

For others with ADHD, the problem is not ignoring coworkers but talking to them too much. Some people with ADHD, particularly those who are extroverts, have a strong need to talk about ideas that have occurred to them. They may become so engrossed in expressing themselves that they ignore the nonverbal people cues that their listener has work to do and would like to terminate the discussion. If you have this problem, here are some coping techniques:

- If you need to talk, go to a place where people interaction is expected (e.g., the lounge or coffee shop).
- Avoid monopolizing the time of support staff and recognize that many have desks in open areas because much of their work requires that they be available to others. Catch yourself if you have a tendency, owing to your ADHD talkativeness, to stretch a friendly greeting into a twenty-minute monologue.
- Write down your ideas.
- Make regular lunch dates at which longer conversations are appropriate.
- Look for work that entails a high degree of interpersonal interaction.

Don't let "Got a minute?" turn into twenty minutes.

Forgetfulness

Not remembering important details others have told you, not remembering to follow through on promises you have made, not remembering to return borrowed items—all of these are typical and unintentional behaviors. Yet they can lead to tremendous resentment on the part of your coworkers if they occur repeatedly. What can you do? Your memory will never become perfect, but there are a number of things you can do to ease the situation (for more suggestions, refer to the section on memory in Chapter 6).

- Ask for things in writing.
- Write things down yourself—in a consistent, well-organized fashion (e.g., by using a day planner).
- Apologize sincerely, and make amends through some small gesture if your memory lapse has negatively affected someone else.

Do it now
or
write it down!

Hyperactivity/Restlessness

Your hyperactivity and restlessness can lead to clear expressions of your impatience with others or of your intolerance of the slow process of group decision making. Some ADHD adults may come across like a bulldozer, pushing people to "get to the point" and badgering them with questions like "What's taking so long?" and exclamations like "Let's go; I don't have all day!" If you recognize yourself in this description, here are some suggestions:

- Look for work that allows a high degree of independent functioning.

- Explain your restlessness with humor so coworkers don't misinterpret it as disinterest.
- Volunteer for those aspects of group projects that require fewer interactive efforts.
- Look for a high-energy work environment.
- Use self-talk and relaxation exercises to calm yourself in situations in which you are likely to become impatient (e.g., meetings).

Disappearing Acts

Restlessness and hyperactivity can also lead to "disappearing acts" at work. Do your boss and coworkers make jokes about never being able to find you? Being on-the-go may be a way you have learned to deal with your ADHD, but if it comes at the expense of your coworkers or if it gives the impression you are goofing off, then you need to find a better coping device. Some suggestions:

- Establish that you really are working but need a change of scenery.
- Obtain permission to go home early or to work in a different part of the building.
- Always tell others where you can be found.
- Be sure to build exercise into each workday.

Social Faux Pas in Meetings

A good deal of the interpersonal interaction in an organization takes place in meetings. To many adults with ADHD, meetings may seem pointless, inefficient, or boring. Some of the most common people faux pas committed by ADHD adults in meetings are the following:

- Becoming argumentative
- Being too blunt or critical when disagreeing with a proposal
- Repeated interrupting

- Tuning out
- Checking your email
- Going off on verbal tangents

Try the following suggestions instead:

- Ask for feedback about your interactions in meetings from a trusted friend or colleague as you try to become aware of and change your problematic habits.
- Take notes at meetings to help slow you down and make you more aware of your thoughts before speaking. Taking notes can also help break a pattern of interrupting for fear you will lose the thought you wanted to express.
- Develop the habit of writing your ideas down before you express them. This will help focus your remarks and avoiding tangents and give you the added time to express yourself more diplomatically.

Launching into Monologues

Some adults with ADHD are prone to give long monologues. Once they launch into a topic, they become totally engrossed and are much less likely to attend to nonverbal cues that their listener has lost interest. Skilled conversation requires flexible shifting, eye contact, and ongoing attention to the other person's responses. If you tend to monologue, try the following:

- Consciously try to speak in short paragraphs—no more than two or three sentences.
- When you catch yourself in a monologue, indicate to your trapped listener that you realize you've gone on far too long, and apologize with humor.
- Ask questions to allow your listener to change the subject.

- Look directly at the other person so you're more likely to catch signs that they would like to respond or that they have lost interest.
- Try to focus on the other person's ideas and paraphrase what you have heard to show you've listened.

Distractibility

Many adults with ADHD are highly distractible. While they are talking with someone at work, their attention may be uncontrollably drawn away by sights and sounds, giving an impression of disinterest. If this happens to you, try the following solutions:

- Apologize and explain that you are easily distracted.
- Suggest going to a less distracting place to continue the conversation.
- Be sure to give your coworkers the impression that you are interested in what they say.
- Suggest a specific time to continue the discussion if a coworker catches you when you are preoccupied.
- Seat yourself so you will be less distracted by the movement of others in the room.

Are You Prone to "Tell It Like It Is"?

Bluntness is saying the first thing that comes to mind without considering the possible consequences. Some adults with ADHD, unfortunately, congratulate themselves on their "honesty" instead of recognizing the harm they may do to others—and the harm they are doing to themselves in the process. It is quite possible to be direct and honest without being destructively critical, angry, or belittling. Follow these steps:

- First, recognize that your bluntness is seldom valued as refreshing candor.

- Practice slowing down your responses in conversations. Give yourself time to stop and think.
- Do some advance planning. If you need to broach a particularly sensitive topic with a coworker, think about what you'd like to say, write it down, and possibly even discuss your approach with someone else in order to find a constructive way to discuss a touchy subject.
- If bluntness is the result of frustration or anger, remove yourself until you feel more calm.

Hypersensitivity to Criticism

Ironically, although some ADHD adults can be blunt with others, they themselves are often hypersensitive to criticism or negative feedback. This hypersensitivity results both from a physiological predisposition to overreact emotionally and from a lifetime of criticism for ADHD behaviors. Such hypersensitivity in the workplace can make relationships touchy and difficult.

If a colleague makes a mild complaint and your reaction is one of defensiveness or anger, you have begun to create a relationship in which easy collaboration becomes less and less likely. It is the job of your direct supervisor to give you feedback, both positive and negative. If your reaction to negative feedback is emotional, defensive, or angry, your supervisor will begin to conclude that you are a difficult person to work with. To prevent these consequences, consider the following suggestions:

- If your reactions to criticism are intense, these are issues you may need to work on in therapy.
- Look for work with a supervisor who is calm and supportive.
- Look for ways to solve problems and ease the tensions before strong feelings develop.
- Lower your stress to lower your overreactions.
- Recognize and reduce your contact with people who lead you to overreact.

- Temper reactions in ADHD adults can be triggered by work that requires them to function in an area of weakness for them, causing tension and frustration. Both stress and the overreaction to it are likely to increase when ADHD adults feel they must keep their difficulty in functioning secret.
- Avoid or minimize tasks that are difficult and frustrating; you're more prone to emotional reactions when functioning in an area of weakness.

Destress yourself so you don't distress others.

Difficulty Accepting Guidance or Direction from Others

Some but not all adults with ADHD strongly prefer to operate independently; these individuals often experience great difficulty in accepting guidance or direction. ADHD adults who choose to work alone run a risk, however, if they also have poor organizational skills and/or a strong tendency to procrastinate. Finding the ideal balance between freedom and structure can prove difficult. Some ADHD adults achieve this balance by collaborating with a well-selected business partner or office manager; not infrequently, the spouse fills this role.

There are some fields in which there is no choice but to work in tandem with others and under the supervision of others. If you are in this position, here are some approaches you can take that may lessen your discomfort:

- The most important comfort factor lies in the match between yourself and your supervisor. If your supervisor seems overly critical or controlling, the best approach may be to seek a different position within the same organization with a supervisor who can provide structure while also being supportive.

- Depending on the strength of your reaction to feeling "micromanaged," the nature of your supervisor may be one of the most important factors to consider in looking for a good job match.
- Even in group projects, there are certain tasks that require less interaction and coordination with others. Look for and request such tasks.
- Examine your own reactions to supervision. You may be able to alter defensive reactions to improve relations between you and your supervisor.

Conclusion

This chapter has discussed a range of potential interpersonal glitches that may be caused by certain types of ADHD traits and reactions. The following points are intended as a general summary of ways to improve your interpersonal functioning in the workplace.

1. **Explain yourself.**

   Don't make excuses.

   Recognize your effect on coworkers.

   Explain that your patterns of reaction are sometimes out of your control.

   Most importantly, explain that you are making efforts to change those patterns.

2. **Catch yourself.** Just because you become aware of patterns doesn't mean they will automatically disappear! Don't become overly critical of yourself when you repeat problematic patterns. Just try to catch yourself and make a midcourse correction.

3. **Apologize.** When you catch yourself doing something that may have bothered a coworker, acknowledge it and apologize. It is

much easier for others to feel tolerant and supportive of ADHD adults who are aware and concerned about their effect on their coworkers.

4. **Develop positive habits.** Don't just focus on the negative. Deliberately look for positive interpersonal habits that can compensate, in some ways, for negative behaviors not completely under your control. Some adults with ADHD learn these habits instinctively; they use humor, tell entertaining stories, extend friendly greetings, and take the time to pay attention to and do small personal favors for others. If you are genuinely warm and friendly but still have trouble being on time for meetings or turning in your expense report, your ADHD lapses will be balanced in the eyes of others by your efforts to consider them and their feelings.

5. **Look for work that is more independent in nature.** There is tremendous variety in work situations. Some jobs involve close and constant interaction with others, while many other jobs can be performed with a much greater degree of independence. Look for work that provides the right balance between external structure and support on the one hand and freedom to do your own thing on the other.

6. **Look for an ADHD–friendly work environment.** Look for an environment in which your ADHD behaviors will be more readily tolerated, for example, (1) where you have more independence, (2) where you are not closely supervised or required to work closely with others, (3) where the atmosphere is more casual, and (4) where the product is more important than the process. Workplace environments that are more casual and less rule bound are more likely to tolerate aberrations on your part. But remember, no matter where you work—and even if you work only with your spouse—you cannot assume that anything goes and that you don't need to worry about your effect on others. Even the tolerance level of a loyal spouse can be surpassed!

Actively Work to Build Positive Relationships

Much of what has been discussed in this chapter focuses on what *not* to do, that is, don't ignore, don't interrupt, don't argue, don't procrastinate, and so forth. It's just as important to focus on what *to do* at work. Let's start with the overall importance of "playing well with others"—we are graded on this as early as preschool and kindergarten, and the importance of getting along with others never diminishes. If you just focus on the fact that this is an important part of doing your job well, that's half the battle. Getting along at work relies on tried-and-true actions:

1. Be friendly—smile, say hello, introduce yourself.
2. Remember names—if this is hard for you in a meeting or on a new job assignment, then write the names down with some reminder so you'll know whose name it is. At meetings, it can be helpful to write down names according to the position at which they sit around the table.
3. Be helpful and generous—ask if there is a way to reduce someone's workload if they have been sick or have had a family crisis.
4. Do what you've promised—avoid forgetfulness by writing reminders. Sending yourself an e-mail reminder is a simple way to keep track of small tasks.
5. Be a team player—stay late if others are doing so to meet an important deadline.
6. Communicate *before* little problems become big ones.

Work on these habits until they become just that—habitual. It can be very helpful to work with an ADHD coach while you are working on developing better people skills.

A Final Note on People Skills

Many adults with ADHD have excellent people skills and are drawn into careers that take full advantage of them. Other adults with ADHD, those who may experience difficulties and frustration in a corporate environment, are enormously successful in the entrepreneurial world, where they have more freedom, autonomy, and opportunity to create a work world that stimulates and challenges them in positive ways.

Don't be too hard on yourself. People skills are habits that take repeated practice. With a sense of humor about your foibles, with a genuine desire to get along with others, and perhaps with the assistance of a counselor or therapist, you can make good progress toward improving your on-the-job relationships.

Note

1 Hyatt, C., & Gottlieb, L. (2009). *When Smart People Fail.* New York: Simon & Schuster.

This chapter focuses on aspects of the work environment that can either help or hinder you. Whether you are trying to make improvements in your current job or are looking for a new job, the discussion in this chapter can help you.

10

An ADHD–Friendly Work Environment

The key to finding an ADHD–friendly work environment begins with understanding yourself and your needs. Different individuals with ADHD have different needs. This book is designed to help you have a clear, strong sense of your individual needs so you can find or create a work environment in which most of your needs are met.

An ADHD–friendly work environment is one that enhances your ability to function at your best. A number of factors—both physical and interpersonal—come into play. Your relationship with your boss or immediate supervisor is certainly one of the most important factors (more about this in the next chapter).

As an adult with ADHD, you need to take responsibility for yourself, your choices, and for advocating for your needs on the job. It is *not* the responsibility of your employer to create an ideal environment for you or to understand the accommodations you may need. If you are thinking about asking for accommodations under the Americans with Disabilities Act, it is your responsibility to understand your own needs (ideally with the help of a professional with expertise in ADHD workplace accommodations) and then request "reasonable" accommodations of your employer. In my experience in working with many adults with ADHD, employees who make themselves valuable assets in their workplace are much more likely to receive accommodations that are provided willingly and informally. However, many things that cause a particular job to be ADHD friendly have nothing to do with formal accommodations. In this chapter, we'll explore what those factors are.

Reasonable Stress Levels

Stress can't be entirely avoided. All jobs entail some level of stress, and workplace stress seems to be on the rise as employers try to accomplish more with fewer employees. The stress level of your job is critical to your satisfaction and success on the job, because adults with ADHD are more susceptible to stress than their non-ADHD colleagues are.[1] High stress increases ADHD symptoms. In fact, an increase in ADHD patterns such as forgetfulness and disorganization are among the first signs of stress. You may think that you are coping well during a particularly demanding period at work, but then suddenly you realize that you are forgetting more things, are less organized, and are letting things slip through the cracks. During periods when your ADHD seems worse, the first culprit to look for is stress.

How is stress created? Although the same things are not stressors for all people, the following are common stressors on the job:

Stress Factors on the Job
Long hours
A long commute in heavy traffic
Fear of being fired
Fear for the company's future
New management
Crisis-style management

Stress Factors on the Job *(continued)*
A supervisor with a high-criticism, low-praise management style
Unrealistic demands for high productivity
Poor communication and collaboration in the workplace
Unclearly defined duties and responsibilities
Conflicts with coworkers
Promotion to a management position
Work that calls on you to work primarily in areas of weakness

We are only focusing here on workplace stressors, but stressors in your personal life can also have a negative impact on your ADHD symptoms at work. These should be monitored and managed as well. Your performance at work will almost certainly suffer if you are under great strain at home due to financial concerns, chronic illness of a family member, marital stress, or parenting stress. Parenting stress is often higher for adults with ADHD because they are likely to have one or more children with ADHD who present special needs and challenges.

Low stress
=
ADHD friendly

Coping with High Stress Levels at Work

In worst-case scenarios, when your job is hugely stressful, the best solution may be to look for a different job. But before taking that step, the first thing to do is to identify the major sources of stress and then problem solve. If you love your job but have a long, grueling commute, it may be wise to consider moving closer to your work, if that is feasible. If communication is poor between your manager and your team, you may be able to address that directly by asking for more regular team meetings, for example. If the demand for productivity is unrealistic, it may be helpful to talk to coworkers to explore whether they are experiencing the same thing. Then talk to your managers about the issue. In other words, work in a proactive, problem-solving mode to look for ways to reduce identified sources of stress.

Optimal Stimulation

Stress should not be confused with stimulation. Stress refers to things that are distressing, whereas a stimulating job challenges you, piques your interest, and gets your juices flowing. Ideal levels of stimulation can reduce ADHD symptoms. Each person has his or her own "window of optimal stimulation." When workplace stimulation falls below that window, boredom and lethargy can set in. When stimulation levels at work exceed your window, stimulation morphs into stress. It is important to understand your optimal level of stimulation and to learn ways to remain inside your "optimal window" as much as possible.

When stimulation levels are ideal, you are more likely to function in a focused, creative, and effective fashion. However, stimulation is a double-edged sword. While optimal stimulation can reduce ADHD symptoms and maximize effectiveness, overstimulation can become stress and can increase your ADHD symptoms. Sometimes overstimulation is self-inflicted. For example, those with ADHD fortunate enough to work in a field of high interest may eagerly take on new projects without considering whether they really have the time for them.

How would you rate the stimulation level of your current job? In most jobs, the stimulation level varies. Your goal should be to find or create a job that has the right level of stimulation most of the time. It may help to review all of your previous jobs and to rate each of them in terms of stimulation. Here are some things that might be helpful to think about as you consider the stimulation level of your current job:

- Your level of interest in the job
- Opportunity for creativity
- Degree of challenge presented by your job
- Opportunity to learn new skills
- Degree of interaction with others
- Opportunity for travel
- Pace of work
- Degree of freedom to pursue your own interests

UNDERSTIMULATION
=
Repetitive, Routine, Boring

OPTIMAL STIMULATION
=
Challenging, Interesting, Engaging

OVERSTIMULATION
=
Overwhelming, Exhausting, Frenzied

Stimulation and Personality Type

What is stimulating varies from person to person, according to interests and personality type (see Chapter 5, "ADHD and Personality Type at Work").[2]

If you are not sure of your personality type, you may find it helpful to take the Myers-Briggs Type Indicator so you can take your type into account as you think about how to create your optimal stimulation zone at work.

Extroversion–Introversion

Extroverts (Es) need people interaction to function optimally. Es who are isolated run the risk of slumping into the "understimulation zone," where they may experience boredom and restlessness and are prone to underfunctioning. Introverts (Is), by contrast, should guard against too much interpersonal interaction that may push them into the "overstimulation zone," where ADHD symptoms worsen.

Sensing–Intuition

Sensors (Ss) function best when they are busy accomplishing practical things—making, fixing, building, curing, or solving practical problems. Ss often find it very satisfying to do things with their hands. An S will not be stimulated by an "all talk and no action" environment. Intuitives (Ns), on the other hand, are most stimulated by the world of ideas, the world of the possible rather than the actual. Ns are stimulated when they are imagining, writing, creating, and thinking.

Thinking–Feeling

Thinkers (Ts) love to analyze in a detached, problem-solving fashion. A group of Ts may feel wonderfully stimulated as they work to understand why a machine is malfunctioning or how a certain economic formula may be applied. This same group of Ts, however, may feel terribly stressed when the problem that needs solving involves people and feelings. The people-oriented problems that are typically stressful to Ts are life's blood to Feelers (Fs), who are most stimulated by working with people, by empathizing, helping, and doing something "meaningful." Fs would feel detached and understimulated if they did work that involved only things instead of people.

Judging–Perceiving

Judgers (Js) thrive on structure and will try to create it if it isn't provided in the work environment. Js tend to find an unpredictable work environment highly stressful and distracting, whereas organization and structure help them find their zone of optimal stimulation. Perceivers (Ps) are in their optimal zone when they have the freedom to be spontaneous and flexible. In a highly structured, rigid work environment, Ps will feel confined and unable to "be themselves." Ps are drawn to work that is flexible in hours, and that allows them to respond more according to mood and less according to plan. Ps often thrive in work that allows them to work all night if they are inspired and doesn't hold them to a rigid work schedule.

ADHD Traits and Optimal Stimulation

In addition to personality factors, a number of ADHD traits vary from one adult to another and strongly influence how much and what type of stimulation is ideal at work.

Routine and Predictability

While some adults with ADHD greatly rely on structure and routine to manage their ADHD symptoms, other adults with ADHD have little tolerance for routine. Their needs for change and challenge may result in frequent job changes. These individuals love the challenge and creativity involved in developing a program or product, but they become bored or frustrated with the day-to-day operations of maintaining what they have created. Thom Hartmann talks about this phenomenon among entrepreneurs with ADHD and strongly counsels them to plan on turning over the day-to-day operations of their enterprises to a managerial type.[4]

If you are someone that needs routine and predictability in order to function well at work, you probably won't feel comfortable in a free-wheeling start-up or in a company whose leadership is shaky due to a merger or buyout. On the other hand, if you are hungry for change and challenge, then too much predictability on the job may make it nearly intolerable.

Opportunity for Physical Movement

As you may be aware, the activity level of adults with ADHD varies hugely, from couch potatoes who have trouble initiating any activity to adults on the hyperactive end of the movement spectrum who are happiest when in motion. If you crave movement, you'll feel better in work that allows or requires you to stand and move periodically throughout the day.

I worked with one very bright young woman, a recent college grad with a degree in economics from a highly competitive university. She came to Washington, DC for her first job but was soon very unhappy because her work required her to sit motionless in front of a computer all day. Upon my advice, she asked her supervisor for permission to take an activity break periodically throughout the day so that she could take the elevator to the ground floor and speed-walk around the block before returning to her desk. Other desk jockeys with ADHD are requesting a standing desk or, better yet, a desk that allows them to walk on a treadmill while working at their computer. The young woman who needed activity breaks rapidly concluded that she needed to pursue a different type of employment and returned to school to become certified as a teacher—a job that would allow her to stand in front of her class and move about the classroom throughout the day.

One man with ADHD developed his own private demolition company. He loved the risk, the movement, the rough-and-tumble interaction with the men who worked under him. Another action-oriented ADHD adult went into the car auction

(story continued)
business. Crisscrossing several states in his region of the country, he bought cars at auction and resold them to local dealers. He loved the irregular schedule, the easy social interaction with other men at the auctions, and the challenge of quickly judging the worth of a car and making a shrewd bargain.

Yet another man with ADHD held a job as the head of a construction crew employed by a national franchise. The crew's task was to completely remodel shopping center space to the specifications of the company within a period of three to five days. This ADHD adult liked the variety and challenge inherent in quickly designing and building each space to meet the specifications of the franchisee. Like other restless, hyperactive individuals with ADHD, he liked alternating between intense periods of work punctuated by slack time between jobs.

Social Stimulation

Social stimulation is essential for extroverted adults with ADHD. Sales, lobbying, politics, entertainment, and public relations all hold appeal for ADHD adults who have a strong need for social stimulation. One woman with ADHD earned a degree in chemistry. However, once she was in the workplace, she soon realized that she was very unhappy with the social isolation of her work. After a couple years, she decided to use her intelligence and analytical abilities in a completely new career as a financial advisor—a job that allowed her to frequently interact with her clients.

Understanding Your Ideal Sources of Stimulation

Of course, there are adults with ADHD who are drawn to combinations of various sources of stimulation. One young woman, for example, finally chose to leave the academic environment, which she had found too sedentary and frustrating, to enter the world of haute cuisine. There she found a combination of physical activity, social interaction, opportunity for creativity, and constant new challenges.

As you consider ways to try to change your current job or seek a new job, it's important for you to have a clear understanding of the types of stimulation you need to function at your best.

Chris, an adolescent with ADHD, had an incredible stroke of luck when his family arranged for him to become a page on Capitol Hill in Washington, DC during his high school years. Because he was extremely restless and had little interest in academics, he would probably have done poorly in a typical high school environment. On Capitol Hill, however, the pages attend high school for only a few hours each morning and then spend the remainder of their day talking, interacting, and running errands for busy senators and representatives. It was a perfect environment for him. Rather than attending college, he remained on Capitol Hill, where he was widely known and admired, and worked his way into higher levels of employment on the strength of his energy, personality, and experience.

Freedom from Distraction

The level of distraction in your work environment can make or break your ability to perform well. Studies have shown that even among non–ADHD adults, distractions can significantly reduce productivity.

Even normal levels of distraction, however, can prove difficult for those with ADHD. It's important to look for a work environment that is as nondistracting as possible. In the modular or open office environment so common today, freedom from distraction is not easy to achieve.

One of the most challenging sources of distraction is Internet access. As boredom sets in, it's all too easy to fall into a pattern of checking the scores of your favorite team, messaging your friends, or doing a bit of online shopping. Studies have shown that the best time to send out Twitter messages is 4 p.m.—the time that most workers are fatigued from the day and are seeking a respite from their workday. For those with ADHD, the Internet may beckon throughout the day if they are bored or having trouble getting started on a difficult task. One way to reduce the lure of the Internet is to position your monitor so that it will be in clear view of coworkers and those passing by. If others are potentially aware of what you're doing, that may provide the level of accountability that will keep you on task at work.

Other common workplace distractions come from:

- Conversations and phone calls of coworkers
- People passing by your desk
- General noise pollution from the operation of office equipment
- Visual clutter

Creating a Calm, Quiet, Less Distracting Work Space

The ideal setting for some adults with ADHD is a private office. For most workers, however, this is not an option. If you work in a modular environment, ask for a cubicle out of the line of traffic. Seek a cubicle that is not near the photocopying machine, the water fountain, the boss's office, or along the main corridor down which everyone walks. If you lack even the benefit of a modular office space, you can request portable screens to surround your desk on three sides to cut down on both visual and auditory distractions.

Noise pollution can be diminished through the use of headphones or a small white-noise machine near your desk. Visual distraction can be minimized by placing your desk chair facing away from the opening to your cubicle. Other important visual distractors, however, may be found within your own cubicle!

Even non–ADHD adults tend to work more efficiently when they work in a neat, orderly work space with a clean desktop. If visual clutter creates distraction for you, it may be very helpful to request help from a professional organizer to help you declutter and organize your work area.

Interruptions

It's difficult enough for adults with ADHD to stay on track at work, but when interruptions occur, it can become almost impossible. Even for adults without ADHD, interruptions are a huge time thief. By the time your coworker has left after a ten-minute chat about something completely unrelated to what you were doing, it will take you ten to fifteen minutes before you are fully re-engaged with what you were doing, which means that each interruption costs you twenty or more minutes of productive time. And what's even more challenging is that if you have ADHD, it's quite likely that you *won't* get back to the task you were engaged in because something else has caught your attention in the meanwhile. Perhaps you jump onto a task your coworker has mentioned that needs to be done. (Adults with ADHD tend to be more reactive—i.e., responsive to requests from others—rather than proactive in charting a course for the day's tasks.)

Interruptions might occur due to a phone call, a visitor, a coworker, a ping from your e-mail, or a meeting. The layout of your work environment will give you a strong clue regarding how frequent interruptions may be, but you'll need to be proactive in guarding against interruptions that can be better managed—by setting aside specific times of day to check e-mail; by looking for an unused conference room when you're working on a task that requires extended concentration, and by talking to your supervisor about avoiding nonessential meetings.

The interruption of phone calls can be minimized by taking all your calls as voicemail and then setting aside blocks of time to return calls at your own convenience instead of allowing random incoming calls to interrupt your work and destroy your concentration. One man with ADHD had to make an additional accommodation for a boss who needed to be able to contact him immediately rather than resort to voicemail: He carried a beeper that signaled him that his boss had called so he could return the call immediately.

Telecommuting as a Way to Reduce Distractions and Interruptions

An increasing number of employers allow telecommuting one or more days per week, and some employers even allow full-time telecommuting, only requiring employees to be on hand for meetings and other group events. While working from home may help you avoid the distractions of the workplace, most home environments contain an even greater number of distractions. The tasks of daily life call to someone working from home—"I'll just take a few minutes to put in a load of laundry; I'll straighten up the kitchen now, or maybe start dinner early so that it will be ready when everyone comes home hungry." Not to mention that home is filled with more appealing distractions such as television and the Internet, or running a quick errand that ends up taking an hour or more. If your goal is to work from home in order to complete an important task that requires uninterrupted focus, you'll need to create a workplace within your home that helps structure you and keep you on track (more about this in Chapter 14).

Time-Shift Your Work Hours to Avoid Distractions and Interruptions

Meetings and casual interruptions are essential to manage if you are to function efficiently in the workplace as an adult with ADHD. One way to enhance work efficiency is to arrive early or stay late so you have a block of time each day with few, if any, interruptions. If you are working on an important project, ask permission to be absent from nonessential meetings so your train of thought isn't broken. It is helpful to develop an automatic, diplomatic way to let people who drop by your office for a quick question or comment know you are busy. Better yet, suggest that they send you e-mail or a memo!

Minimal Paperwork

It is no surprise that paperwork tends to be the bane of the workplace for adults with ADHD. Paperwork entails all the functions that are difficult and frustrating for people with attentional problems, namely attending to detail, organizing thoughts, meeting deadlines, and fighting boredom.

One man with ADHD held a rather high-level government position in which he enjoyed the services of an administrative assistant. Through a departmental reorganization, he lost his assistant. Shortly thereafter, his performance ratings began to decline. The mountains of paperwork, for which the government is well known, became overwhelming. Although he could perform the more complex interpersonal and intellectual aspects of his work, he found himself unable to keep up with paperwork demands. His once promising career deteriorated into an unsatisfying job for which he was ill suited.

Other adults with ADHD have reported similar though less dramatic stories. Keeping track of travel expenses and time sheets is often a chronic point of tension for adults with ADHD.

One young man with ADHD was employed as a social worker in a large social service agency. His job was to interview many people each day to determine their eligibility for various social services. Each client was required to provide a rather large number of documents. The social worker was expected to keep track of each case, to complete all paperwork, and to keep a record of documents that were yet to be provided by each client. After several months on the job, he was hopelessly behind. A mountain of charts lay in complete disarray on his desk. After repeated warnings, he was finally asked to leave his position owing to his inability to keep up with the paperwork. Fortunately, this young man sought treatment for his ADHD. In the course of his therapy, he formulated a plan to seek a job in which he could use his social work training but that had minimal paperwork requirements. He found such work in a psychiatric hospital, where his duties were to interact with patients and staff, lead group meetings, give oral reports on the status of each patient, and write a brief note in each patient's chart at the end of his daily shift. By finding an ADHD–friendly position, he changed from an employee with an unsatisfactory work record to a highly regarded, dedicated staff member.

Needless to say, in seeking an ADHD–friendly job, it is important to look for one in which paperwork is simplified, streamlined, and deemphasized—or, best of all, one in which you can seek the assistance of someone else to keep up with the flow of paperwork!

Short-Term Projects

An important feature of ADHD–friendly work is involvement with projects of limited duration. Complicated, long-term projects can result in diminished interest over time, procrastination, reduced motivation, poor planning, faulty follow-through, and strained organizational skills. Adults with ADHD are often much better suited for more immediate tasks.

> *One woman with ADHD had a job that involved responding immediately to incoming telephone calls. Each caller had specific questions that had to be researched and responded to on the spot. There was no opportunity for procrastination, no requirement to respond to several calls at once, and no possibility of becoming forgetful or disorganized. The woman described this as the perfect job for her ADHD. She always had something immediate and different to stimulate her, and there was no left-over paperwork at the end of the day.*

Help with Long-Term Projects

Long-term projects that require planning and organizational skills are often the downfall of adults with ADHD. If you are in a job with a strong emphasis on such projects, your best approach is to emphasize teamwork so individuals better suited to the planning and monitoring of the project can take major responsibility for those aspects, leaving you freer to focus on problem solving (often an ADHD strength) or on short, clearly defined aspects of the long-term project.

An ADHD–friendly job that entails long-term projects will provide the following:

- Clearly defined short-term tasks.
- Regular (weekly, perhaps even daily) feedback from a supervisor
- Teamwork with someone more skilled in long-term planning

"Big Picture" Emphasis

The ideal ADHD–friendly job is one in which the "big picture" skills of the adult with ADHD are emphasized and the details are left to a more focused, detail-oriented non–ADHD individual. Hard-to-manage details often include:

- Scheduling
- Paperwork requirements
- Multistep bureaucratic procedures
- Keeping track of addresses and phone numbers
- Filing

Limited Supervisory Responsibility

Being promoted to a position that requires the supervision and management of others can be the downfall of an adult with ADHD because such a position requires one to monitor and guide others, attend to details, and assume multiple, sometimes competing responsibilities. These tasks tend to be difficult for adults with ADHD who have difficulty with self-monitoring and in attending to the details of their own work. When the responsibility for others is added, they may become overwhelmed and disorganized.

Promotions Can Be a Downfall

The promotion, the raise, and the prestige are often temptations too strong to resist. ADHD adults who have worked hard to become experts in their field often find that when they are promoted to management, they shift from peak functioning to faltering. They have moved into a position that calls on their weaknesses rather than their strengths.

There are certainly ADHD people whose symptoms are mild or whose compensatory skills are excellent who can do an adequate or even good job as a manager. If you decide to accept such a position, though, it is important that you recognize the potential pitfalls. If you have made your best efforts and find the job still isn't right for you, don't try to hang in there no matter what. Recognize the problem for what it is, namely, a job that emphasizes your areas of weakness, and head for a more ADHD–friendly position.

Breaks from Extended Concentration

Long conferences and half-day or all-day meetings are extremely tiring and stressful for those with ADHD. They typically surpass the concentration span of non–ADHD adults, too. An ADHD–friendly job rarely requires the individual to focus and concentrate for such long periods without opportunity for breaks. If you are in a job in which such meetings are inevitable, arrange to take brief breaks independently if enough breaks are not scheduled during the meeting. In addition, some adults with ADHD find that their attention span is extended if they take notes during the meeting.

ADHD–Friendly Physical Environment

An ADHD–friendly physical environment has good lighting, clean air, and a comfortable temperature; is reasonably quiet, spacious, and orderly; and includes a comfortable desk and chair. People with ADHD are sometimes hypersensitive to certain aspects of their physical environment, aspects that may be only minor irritants to others. If this is true for you, there is no need to feel defensive or apologetic; often there is a neurological basis for this type of hypersensitivity. Hypersensitive children, for example, may be extremely irritated by wool or scratchy material and even by labels and seams in their clothing. Such hypersensitivity may be due to problems with what is called sensory integration.

You may find that you are bothered by loud sounds or by sounds at certain pitches. Some people with ADHD are extra sensitive to the flickering of fluorescent lighting. Irritants in the physical work environment all take their toll, increasing fatigue, distractibility, and other ADHD symptoms. Don't condemn yourself as being too picky if you find you are more sensitive than your coworkers to environmental irritants; you're not being picky, you're being ADHD smart.

Conclusion

To sum it all up, many important factors in combination create an ADHD–friendly work environment.

A Quick Checklist of ADHD–Friendly Job Characteristics

1. Manageable stress levels
2. Optimal stimulation suited to your personality type
3. Nondistracting workspace
4. Minimal paperwork
5. Mostly short-term projects
6. Assistance with long-term projects
7. Emphasis on the "big picture"—not on details
8. Limited supervisory duties
9. Opportunity for movement/breaks from demand for concentration
10. Comfortable physical environment
11. High-interest activity

No workplace environment is perfect. It is unreasonable to ask for perfection, but you should take your reactions to the work environment seriously. Think about yourself and your current job in terms of the ADHD–friendly workplace factors listed in this chapter. Can you think of creative ways to reduce and minimize problems? Perhaps this chapter will give you ideas of ways to improve your current job as well as things to look for in your next job.

Notes

1 Kroeger, O., & Thuesen, J. (2009). *Type Talk at Work: How the 16 Personality Types Detetmine Your Success on the Job.* New York: Random House, LLC.
2 Hartmann, T. (2010). *ADHD Secrets of Success: Coaching Yourself to Fulfillment in the Business World.* New York: SelectBooks.

If you have an opportunity to make a transfer within your company or if you are in the process of looking for a new job, this chapter can offer a few guidelines for seeking a good fit between you and your new supervisor.

11

What to Look for in a Boss

Why Fantasize about an Ideal Boss?

"Why think about an ideal boss if I'm stuck with the one I have?" At several points in this book, parallels have been drawn between workplace issues for adults with ADHD and school issues for children with ADHD. Here is another important parallel: Just as children often have little or no choice of teacher, adults have little latitude in choosing a supervisor. Nevertheless, it is an important issue to consider for several reasons.

First, you won't always be working under your current supervisor. You may transfer or leave your job, and your supervisor may do likewise. Second, believe it or not, some supervisors are motivated to become better supervisors! Your current supervisor has probably had no training in how best to work with an adult with ADHD. Owing to lack of information, he or she may have developed approaches that are uncomfortable or ineffective for you. If you have a reasonably positive relationship with your supervisor, you may be able to communicate some of the information contained in this chapter to him or her and develop a dialogue that leads to a more productive relationship.

Third, when you do have a choice—that is, when you are job hunting, either within your current organization or somewhere else—you will know which qualities to look for.

Who Is the Ideal Supervisor for an Adult with ADHD?

A better question to ask is "What's *my* ideal supervisor like?" Not all people with ADHD are alike. Some need a high degree of structure and predictability in a supervisor; others flourish under a more laissez-faire management style. Some people with ADHD are hypersensitive to stress and need a calm, predictable work environment; others crave stimulation and variety and would find such an environment boring. Nevertheless, there are certain characteristics to be found among great bosses and others that define "bosses from hell."

ADHD Tales from the Workplace

A Boss from Hell

John was a bright computer whiz who was highly regarded in a rapidly growing high-tech company. Because of his expertise in software development and his engaging manner, he was targeted for a promotion that involved public relations and new product development.

> *John's problems began shortly after he started work in his new position. Unfortunately, his new boss was somewhat insecure and had relatively little supervisory experience. He misinterpreted John's easygoing style as laziness, his ADHD*

(story continued)

forgetfulness as irresponsibility, his need to shift from one task to another in order to maintain interest and motivation as disorganization, and his ideas and suggestions for change as a direct challenge to his authority as a supervisor.

John's performance deteriorated under the tension, lack of support, and frequent criticisms from his boss. The more depressed and discouraged he became, the less he was able to function. His boss's style was to focus on his supervisees' inadequacies and to rarely, if ever, emphasize things that were going well.

As his morale sank to dangerous levels, John sought ADHD–oriented career counseling. He requested that his psychologist write a letter clearly outlining the types of assistance and accommodations he needed at work.

Unfortunately, this supervisor didn't "believe" in ADHD and felt angry that he was required under the Americans with Disabilities Act to provide accommodations. His approach was to adhere to the letter but not the spirit of the recommendations.

John wasn't fired, but his supervisor clearly intended to make him want to resign. After several months of unbearable tension between them, John realized it was futile to continue to attempt to gain his boss's support and confidence.

What were the characteristics of this supervisor that made him an "ADHD boss from hell"? John's supervisor was:

- Nonsupportive
- Inflexible
- Overfocused on details
- Prone to misinterpret ADHD symptoms

- Unaware of the strengths his supervisee brought to the job
- Highly controlling
- Threatened by his supervisee's questions and requests
- Uninformed and didn't "believe in" ADHD
- Resentful at being asked to make accommodations for ADHD symptoms
- Overfocused on the negative

Fear of enduring an experience like John's is what makes many adults with ADHD reluctant to disclose their disorder. Such reactions are not universal, however. And, more importantly, there are many things you can do without formally disclosing your ADHD diagnosis to improve your work environment. Now let's take a look at a supervisory relationship that worked beautifully.

An Ideal ADHD Supervisor

Ann was a middle-aged woman who returned to full-time work after raising her children. Although she was a college graduate, she had always had difficulty in school without knowing why and had found school very stressful. Only years later, after the evaluation of a son who was diagnosed with ADHD and learning problems, did Ann come to understand that she had struggled with ADHD without benefit of diagnosis or treatment.

Ann decided to seek testing and treatment to smooth her reentry into the workplace environment.

Ann was hired as an administrative assistant to one of the deans at a local university. She was selected because of her obvious intelligence, excellent verbal skills, and warm, caring manner. The dean, who was looking for someone who would serve as a "welcoming committee" for the many people who sought contact with her in person and on the phone, immediately recognized Ann's people skills.

An Ideal ADHD Supervisor *(continued)*

Although Ann loved her job, her ADHD began to create problems from the start. She never developed an effective filing system and soon was forced to waste long periods of time searching for memos and letters. Ann made typos and careless spelling errors (only some of which were caught by the computer's spell checker). She had little computer training and found the computer to be rather intimidating.

Any of these problems could have led to disaster, but no disaster occurred. Why? Because Ann had the good fortune to have an enlightened boss. The dean, as chance would have it, was familiar with the issues relating to ADHD. She was also impressed with Ann's maturity, people skills, and forthright approach to stating her problems and seeking solutions.

Ann worked with another dean's assistant to learn how to develop a better filing system. Ann attended classes to master the computer program she used on a daily basis. A student came in for several hours a week to assist Ann with typing and filing, thus allowing Ann to focus more comfortably on her people-related tasks.

The dean had found in Ann someone who could present a warm, professional, engaging face to the world and helped her find the accommodations and supports she needed in order to concentrate on her strengths.

What were the characteristics of this boss that made her an ideal match for an ADHD adult? The dean was:

- Supportive
- Flexible
- Focused on her employee's strengths
- Knowledgeable about ADHD symptoms

- Confident in herself and comfortable enough with an employee to find solutions
- Not prone to power struggles
- Respectful toward her employee
- Creative in finding solutions to problems
- Prone to emphasize positive traits

"Okay," you might say, "but how many bosses are like Ann's?" Good question. Not most, unfortunately. However, thinking about Ann's boss can give you guidelines for some of the characteristics you'd like to find in a supervisor. You might not find someone with all the characteristics of Ann's boss, but you may have the good fortune to find someone who is flexible and motivated to learn how to best work with you.

Working with the Boss You Have

Don't expect your boss to figure you out. It's up to you to teach your boss how to best work with you. In other words, you have to know what you need and how you work best. When you are looking for a new job, your focus should be on finding a supervisor who you think will be a good match. If you already have a job, you need to help your supervisor understand you and your needs, and you need to teach him or her how to help you work most effectively.

Working Effectively with Your Boss

There are many positive, constructive ways to talk about your ADHD symptoms and to work constructively with your boss to seek solutions. Here are some guidelines:

- Respect your boss's time and efforts. He or she has many responsibilities; supervising you is only one of them. Don't demand too much of your boss's time and energy. Regular, scheduled, focused, and brief supervisory sessions often are most effective.

- Don't let problems become enormous before you talk about them.
- Address your difficulties early—and in a positive, constructive fashion.
- Don't just talk about your challenges; introduce possible solutions at the same time.
- Don't throw the problem into your boss's lap and expect him or her to solve it. You need to become informed enough about your ADHD to propose reasonable solutions.
- In many cases, it is best not to disclose an ADHD diagnosis but to simply discuss problems and solutions in the context of the situation.

Searching for a More ADHD-Friendly Boss

"How do I know what a new supervisor is really like until I work for him or her?" Job hunting is a two-way street. When you are interviewing for a new position, your prospective employer will do his or her best to find out about you—by reading your resume, talking with you, observing you, and speaking to your references. Employers do everything they can to make an accurate prediction about the type of employee an interviewee will become.

You need to engage in the same process. Don't just worry about whether they will like you. You also need to think about whether you will like them. You should do just as much research as your prospective employer in order to determine whether the job and the supervisor will be a good fit for you.

It's important for you to know what you're looking for and to feel comfortable asking questions about management style, the general atmosphere at work, turnover rate in the department, and the organizational structure of the company. If possible, find out whether the company is in the process of change; if there has been a merger or if one is anticipated in the near future, a change in structure and hierarchy is inevitable.

Use as many sources as you can to learn about your prospective employer. Look for friends or acquaintances who work for the firm or who know someone who does. Do some research on the internet if you are considering a nationwide firm.

The Characteristics of Your Own Ideal Boss

When you are seeking the right boss, you should consider not only your ADHD characteristics but also your personality in more general terms. Don't get so over-focused on your ADHD symptoms that you overlook your personality, your interests, and your values. It is sometimes helpful to think about the Myers-Briggs personality types (see Chapter 5) when you try to imagine the type of person who would make an ideal boss for you. Entire books have been written about the Myers-Briggs Type Indicator (MBTI). It would be impossible within the confines of this chapter to offer a complete discussion of the MBTI (however, the discussion in Chapter 5 is a more complete one, and you may want to refer to it before continuing). Here, in the context of considering your ideal boss, we will limit our discussion to a narrow range of personality characteristics.

Ask yourself whether you work best with someone who thinks like you or with someone whose strengths are complementary to yours. There are advantages and disadvantages to either choice.

A Focus on Possibilities Rather Than Immediate Realities

If you are inventive and creative and are always looking for new ways to do things, you may want to look for a supervisor with similar tendencies. In MBTI terms, this means that you are an intuitive (N) personality type and that you are seeking a supervisor who is an N also. Many writers, intellectuals, scientists, professors, and other types of "idea people" are Ns. Those people, with or without ADHD, who are more oriented toward the world of the actual than the possible are sensing (S) rather than intuitive (N) individuals. The majority of people in the world are Ss. Ss are more focused on things that can be felt, touched, and worked with on a practical level. Whether doctors, nurses, engineers, mechanics, or teachers, they are focused on doing their job and improving their skills within the realm of what is already known. Ss rarely stop to think about better ways of doing things; instead, they think in terms of maintaining current procedures in good working order.

If you are an N who is always trying to think of a better way to do things and you are supervised by an S who wants you to just buckle down and do your job, you may experience enormous frustration and tension in the workplace.

An S–N Workplace Vignette

Marcus was a very creative ADHD adult, a strong N on the MBTI. He was hired as a computer specialist in a large, conservative financial organization. The entire organization had a strong S orientation, concerned with preserving the status quo and doing things in a prescribed fashion.

As a result of this enormous difference in orientation, Marcus experienced tremendous frustration each day. Marcus tried, in vain, to explain that things could be done more easily. His suggestions were unwelcome. "Just do your job!" was the attitude of his boss. Meanwhile, Marcus's ADHD tendencies made the constant flow of detailed, repetitive paperwork barely supportable. His performance ratings went from mediocre to poor.

Finally, through counseling, Marcus came to terms with his boss's personality type. He developed a more patient attitude—while he actively looked for another position to which he would be better suited. After several months of discrete exploration, he found a person—another N like himself—who had been placed in

An S–N Workplace Vignette *(continued)*

charge of developing new computer applications for the organization. A few months later, having smoothed out the tension between himself and his current boss, he received a good recommendation and was able to transfer to the more compatible job situation.

Structure versus Flexibility

Another important parameter to consider in terms of both ADHD and the MBTI is your degree of comfort with structure. Don't confuse your difficulty in creating structure with your comfort or discomfort in having structure! In other words, you may be a person whose ADHD leads to somewhat disorganized functioning but who prefers a certain degree of structure. If so, you have a judging (J) rather than a perceiving (P) personality type and might work very well under the supervision of another J who does not have ADHD tendencies toward disorganization.

If you are a P with ADHD—that is, an individual who finds too much structure to be chafing and limiting—you may feel controlled and micromanaged by a J boss. Ps with ADHD typically describe themselves as liking a great degree of freedom and flexibility. Many Ps with ADHD prefer a more "laissez-faire" supervisory style but may greatly benefit from structured assistance provided by support staff.

A P–J Workplace Vignette

Harold was a scientist with ADHD and strong P tendencies who had worked in the academic world for many years, where his P tendencies were comfortably tolerated. As long as he showed up to teach his classes and attend faculty meetings, no one was concerned about his work hours. Harold was a night owl by nature

A P–J Workplace Vignette *(continued)*

(a common trait among people with ADHD). A dedicated and highly creative person, he often worked all night long if he became really involved in an idea he was in the process of developing.

After a number of years in academia, Harold was hired by a private consulting firm. Harold was placed under the supervision of a strong J who had come to the consulting firm from the military—by definition, a strongly J environment, that is, one that values structure, hierarchy, predictability, and punctuality.

Under his J supervisor, Harold's productivity plummeted. Suddenly he was required to arrive at work by 8:30, even if he had been up until 2:00 or 3:00 working on a paper. His J boss was unable to understand why Harold preferred, and actually needed, to work on such a highly variable schedule.

He worked in his own style and at his own pace on evenings and weekends and spent his workday functioning as best he could under the chafing requirements of his J boss. His only hope was that his boss might move on within a year or two and then he might be left in peace by a more flexible supervisor.

Thinking versus Feeling

The thinking–feeling parameter on the MBTI is a critical one to consider in seeking a good match between yourself and your supervisor (as well as a match between yourself and your organization). What is the thinking–feeling parameter? In a general sense, Ts are focused on detached, logical analysis in making decisions, while Fs make decisions along more personal dimensions. One might say that Ts are more focused on non–people-related outcomes (such as research results, inventions, numbers, or the bottom line), whereas Fs are only satisfied when the outcome of their efforts involves and benefits people directly. An F who works under a T might think that the T just doesn't care about people; the T, on the other hand, may think of the F as a "bleeding heart" or as someone quite impractical.

A T–F Workplace Vignette

An F worked under the supervision of a strong T in a social service organization. As is true for many social service organizations, this one was underfunded and understaffed. One day a dictate came down from a state-level administrator that a new software system was to be put into place, requiring that an enormous amount of data be reentered.

The T supervisor, a practical and unsentimental sort, announced that, owing to the press of work demands, the traditional holiday party would consist of an early breakfast rather than the usual luncheon followed by early release from work. This decision was logical in view of the enormous work demands, but it completely ignored the "F" side of the equation—staff morale.

The F employee, a person with good people skills, was able to understand her supervisor's logic. She approached the supervisor on her own terms. She explained that although she understood the pressure the department was under to avoid turning a workday into a holiday, she felt that in the long run, the efficiency and productivity of staff members would decrease if they were deprived of this important time to relax, socialize, and enjoy the holiday spirit. The F's point of view prevailed—because she was able to present her view in terms that could be appreciated by a T supervisor.

Whereas this T–F conflict was resolved in a positive fashion, many such conflicts are not resolved so amiably. For this reason, it is essential that you understand where you fall on the T–F dimension and think about this dimension carefully in choosing both an organization and a supervisor.

Conclusion

As I have tried to demonstrate by using concepts from the MBTI, not every adult with ADHD needs the same thing from a boss. There are some common ingredients, however. In general, you should look for someone who is tolerant of your weaknesses and appreciates your strengths, someone whose motives you trust, whom you feel comfortable communicating with, who can engage with you in creative problem solving, and whose company you enjoy.

"But that's not who I work for!" you point out. First and foremost, you need to be realistic. Before you decide you are in an intolerable situation, take a look at what you can change. You may be surprised by the changes you can bring about in your supervisor by changing your own attitude and approach. Stand back and consider (perhaps with the assistance of a counselor) how you can improve your relationship with your boss. Are there things you could do differently to improve your relationship with him or her (such as getting to work on time and arguing less frequently)? Have you presented your needs in a positive, problem-solving manner and indicated how motivated you are to improve your work performance? Are you positively motivated?

If, after all your efforts, your relationship with your boss remains unsatisfactory, at least you'll have a better idea of what to look for in your next job.

This chapter deals with your legal rights as an adult with ADHD and addresses the often-asked question "Should I disclose my ADHD to my employer?"

12

ADHD and the Americans with Disabilities Act

A law pertinent to adults with ADHD is the Americans with Disabilities Act (ADA).[1] This law requires that employers of more than fifteen employees give employees whose disabilities are documented certain "reasonable accommodations" in order to allow them to perform their work. It also prohibits discrimination against persons on the basis of their disability. It's important that you understand what your rights are and when you should choose, as a last resort, to engage the services of an attorney if you feel the law has not been adhered to.

It Is Your Responsibility to Disclose Your ADHD

Before any laws can be applied to you as an adult with ADHD, you must first inform your employer that you have a disability called attention deficit disorder. The decision to inform an employer is an important one, which we will discuss before going on to outline how the ADA protects adults with ADHD in the workplace.

How to Disclose Your ADHD

Many clients I have worked with have mistakenly thought that mentioning their ADHD to their supervisor was all they were required to do. While disclosure requirements vary from one employer to another, all employers require a disclosure in writing. Such a disclosure is typically make to the HR department of your organization, accompanied by documentation of your disability. Required documentation varies from employer to employer. Some only require a letter from a qualified mental health professional, while others may require a more extensive report that includes test scores documenting ADHD. If you are one of many adults with ADHD that also has one or more learning disorders or cognitive challenges (in reading, writing, math, verbal processing, working memory, processing speed, etc.), it is very likely that you will need up-to-date testing that carefully documents your disorders and outlines how those disorders should be accommodated at work.

Do I Have to Disclose My ADHD?

Some people feel they are being dishonest by not disclosing a disability during a job interview, but you are not required to do so. In fact, it is illegal for a prospective employer to ask about the presence of disability during a job interview. Furthermore, you have no way of knowing how a potential employer might react to such a disclosure. By disclosing, you will almost certainly take yourself out of the running for the job even if you, with reasonable accommodations, would be an excellent choice for it. The employer certainly does not feel obligated to inform you of all the reasons you might not want to accept the job. Neither are you obligated to inform prospective employers of all the reasons they might have for hesitating to hire you. In an interview, both the potential employer and employee are presenting their best selves.

When Should I Disclose My ADHD at Work?

Generally, disclosure is recommended only when other efforts have failed.[1] Why? Because ADHD is an invisible disability that is poorly understood and often interpreted negatively by employers. If you are having difficulty functioning on the job and then decide to disclose your ADHD, you run the risk of being seen in an even more negative light. If you are functioning relatively well on the job but choose to disclose your disability, you may bring about subtle—or not-so-subtle—changes in the way your coworkers view you. This is not always the case. Some people with ADHD who choose to disclose receive a helpful response. You must carefully examine the situation, weighing the pros and cons, before you decide whether to disclose.

Positive Disclosure Experiences

Margaret had difficulty with her immediate supervisor. However, she had developed a warm rapport with her department chief. After repeated attempts to request minor and quite reasonable accommodations from her supervisor, Margaret decided to talk with the chief. She disclosed her ADHD with some trepidation. As luck would have it, the chief responded very supportively, relating in confidence that he was a learning-disabled adult himself. He then worked on Margaret's behalf to influence her supervisor to provide the support she needed on the job.

Negative Disclosure Experiences

In a group discussion at a recent adult ADHD gathering, Joe related his story almost tearfully, warning others to think twice about disclosing their ADHD.

Negative Disclosure Experiences *(continued)*

Joe was a high-ranking executive in a large national corporation when he, along with other managers, was invited to go on a weekend-long executive retreat. Led by a psychologist, group members were encouraged to take personal risks in self-disclosure as an exercise in team building. Joe, entering into the spirit of the occasion, disclosed that he had never been a good student and had only barely graduated from college years before. Working among men who had gone to top colleges, some of whom had gone on to earn graduate degrees in business and law, Joe had never before shared this information about his academic failures. He then went on to disclose that after his son was diagnosed with ADHD, he realized that he had struggled with this disorder all his life. Finally, he disclosed that he was now receiving treatment for ADHD.

Joe was treated and perceived differently almost immediately after the weekend experience. His boss requested an individual meeting to hear more about his ADHD. From that time on, Joe felt that he was gradually shifted out of a position of responsibility. Later, when the company "downsized," Joe was selected to be laid off. Although his suspicions were difficult to document, Joe felt strongly that his being laid off was a direct result of his disclosure during the retreat. Prior to disclosure, he'd had an excellent work record and had received a series of promotions; following his disclosure, his influence and authority were gradually reduced.

Studies are sorely needed on the outcome experienced by people who choose to disclose their ADHD at work. At this point, given general public ignorance about ADHD, especially in adults, it seems reasonable to take a cautious approach and to consider disclosure only when all other avenues have been explored and found lacking.

Alternatives to Disclosure

You don't need to discuss your ADHD in order to ask for reasonable accommodations. Rather than describing your disorder in terms of a disability that needs accommodations, you can just as easily characterize it as a problem that has possible solutions. In this way, you can present yourself in a positive light—as an employee who is trying to become more efficient at work and is seeking support in doing so.

Talk about problems and solutions rather than disability and accommodations.

It may be helpful to refer to Chapter 8, which describes ways to take charge of ADHD patterns at work; there you will find numerous solutions that may be useful to suggest to your supervisor.

When You Should Disclose

In spite of negative experiences like those described earlier in this chapter, there are nevertheless circumstances under which disclosure is warranted.

1. **You should consider disclosing when you feel you will be met by a supportive reaction.** Some fortunate individuals have excellent rapport with their supervisors and feel confident that their value to the firm is well established. If you need accommodations that are unusual enough to require an ADHD disclosure in order to explain your request, this may be an appropriate move.
2. **You should also disclose when all other avenues have been exhausted** and you fear losing your job if you are not granted the accommodations you need. If your reasonable, informal

requests for accommodations have all met with resistance, and your ADHD symptoms seem to be worsening under the stress of changes in the organization or in your job, then disclosure may be your best option.

3. **Finally, you should disclose when you are in danger of losing your job because of poor performance.** In such a case, a disclosure may at least buy you some time. Your employer already has a negative impression. It is possible that the ADHD disclosure may help him or her understand the performance problems you have been demonstrating. No corporation wants to deal with a discrimination suit if they can avoid it. It is much easier for them to go along with your disclosure and your request for reasonable accommodations. They may fire you later, however, after demonstrating that they provided accommodations and your performance remained unsatisfactory. On the other hand, if the accommodations are part of an overall treatment program in which your performance markedly improves, they may be happy to keep you on.

Your Rights under the Law

The preceding section of this chapter has dealt with whether to inform your employer that you have a disability. This section explains briefly exactly how you are legally protected in the workplace as a person with a disability.

Legal Protection under the Americans with Disabilities Act

The Americans with Disabilities Act (ADA)[2] outlaws discrimination against people with disabilities, whether they are employed in the private or public sector (and even extends to people employed by Congress). There are other laws that also pertain to persons with disabilities, but the ADA is by far the most important for workplace issues.

More detailed information about the ADA and other laws can be found online through the Job Accommodations Network (askjan.org) and also through various government websites.

Qualifications for Protection under the ADA

In order to be protected by the ADA in a job discrimination case, you must be able to demonstrate the following:

1. You have a disability.
2. You are "otherwise qualified" to perform the job.
3. You were denied a job or some benefit by reason of your disability.
4. The employer is covered under the ADA.

Let's explore each of these points in detail.

What Qualifies as a Disability under the ADA?

A disability is a physical or mental impairment that substantially limits one or more of a person's major life functions. Some disabilities, such as blindness and deafness, are self-evident. "Invisible" disabilities like ADHD must normally be officially diagnosed by an expert in the field. The expert must provide written documentation of the disability and describe the impairment caused by it. Some employers require both a letter from a physician and a psychological testing report as documentation.

"Otherwise Qualified"

The phrase "otherwise qualified" is critical. You must prove that you are "otherwise qualified" to do the job. That is, you have all the education, experience, know-how, and ability to do the job and would be entirely able to perform the functions involved if you were given certain specified accommodations. There have been cases in which an employer has claimed that the disability itself disqualifies the person to do the job, and this contention has held up in court.

In cases of physical disability, as compared to those involving attentional or learning problems, it is often easier to see how the disabled person can be accommodated in such a way that he or she can perform the job. Moreover, some cases of ADHD affect a majority of areas of functioning, which makes it much more difficult to demonstrate that a person's problems in performing the job would be eliminated if he or she were given certain accommodations.

Denial Strictly on the Basis of Disability

You must be able to demonstrate that your disability was the sole or primary reason you were not selected for the job. An employer is not required to hire you or to retain you because you have a disability. This is an important issue to understand. Some disabled adults, misunderstanding the ADA, believe they can charge an employer with discrimination solely because they were laid off or were not hired in the first place. Your current or potential employer may have a perfectly legitimate reason to prefer someone else over you. Such a preference does not automatically constitute disability discrimination.

Employer Must Be Covered by the ADA

Employers with few employees are not covered by the ADA. This group was excluded because it was felt that the accommodations needed by a person with disabilities would be too costly for a small enterprise. Even in the case of larger enterprises, however, you cannot demand to be granted an unreasonable accommodation (see what follows).

What Is a Reasonable Accommodation?

A reasonable accommodation is an alteration in the employer's work or testing requirements that would enable an individual with a disability to meet the essential requirements of the job without imposing undue hardship on the employer. Which accommodations are deemed reasonable is generally decided on a case-by-case basis when antidiscrimination suits come to court. Over the course of many such cases, precedents will be established for employers to follow. The Job Accommodations Network (JAN),[2] a nonprofit organization, records and categorizes workplace accommodations for all categories of disabilities. You can request from JAN a list of the types of accommodations that are generally considered reasonable for persons with learning disabilities (ADHD is typically lumped together with learning disabilities by the JAN). However, there is no guarantee you will be granted an accommodation just because it has been listed by JAN. (See Chapter 13 for a list of accommodations, which includes many recommended by JAN.)

Taking Legal Action

You need to think about retaining a lawyer when the following conditions exist:

1. You have requested reasonable accommodations, and those requests have been consistently ignored or denied.
2. Your supervisor has begun creating a "paper trail" in apparent preparation for your dismissal without giving you the chance to improve your performance with the benefit of necessary accommodations.
3. You feel strongly that your supervisor has a vendetta against you, is purposely denying reasonable requests from you, and is intentionally making your work life unbearable in order to prompt your resignation. (Beware of this one! When you are

under great stress, it can be easy to misinterpret actions and attitudes.)

4. Your employer has agreed to provide accommodations but is doing so in a nonaccommodating manner. Designed to cause problems, these accommodations adhere to the letter but not the spirit of the law. Situations like this can arise when a company recognizes that it is required to provide accommodations under the ADA and your supervisor has been instructed by a superior to provide such accommodations—for the sole purpose of avoiding a discrimination suit—before dismissing you (or, preferably, prompting your resignation).

Legal action should not be undertaken lightly. Even if you win your case, you should consider what it would be like working for someone whom you have sued. Is this a job you will want? Have you gone through a painful, expensive exercise to vindicate yourself? Is it worth it? Sometimes the answer is "yes." Probably, more often, your money and energies are better spent elsewhere, seeking a different position.

Ron was employed by the federal government as a research scientist. Although a responsible and dedicated employee, Ron suffered, without benefit of diagnosis or treatment, from both ADHD and a written language disability. Although Ron was able to do an excellent job as a researcher in the lab, his ADHD symptoms and language disability led him to experience enormous difficulty in giving presentations and in writing articles for publication.

Ron was eventually diagnosed with ADHD (the learning disability diagnosis came later). He disclosed his ADHD diagnosis to his immediate supervisor, from whom he had received

(story continued)
poor performance ratings. Moreover, Ron was in jeopardy of losing rank as a senior scientist. Unable to maintain a high output of published papers, which was required of a scientist of his rank, he was threatened with a demotion to support scientist. Ron, feeling that he had benefited tremendously from his diagnosis and treatment for ADHD, requested an opportunity to prove his new capacities before being demoted. However, because of the chronic problems with his supervisor, Ron did not receive the accommodations he had requested for his ADHD; furthermore, his supervisor gave him performance requirements that were far beyond the usual, in effect setting him up for failure.

Ron, facing demotion, hired an attorney. An Equal Employment Opportunity Commission (EEOC) hearing was scheduled. All the events were outlined at the hearing, and the panel decided Ron had not been given adequate accommodations for his ADHD or for his newly diagnosed learning disability. Additionally, the panel found that the requirements placed on Ron to keep his job were unreasonable. Accommodations and a change in requirements were ordered, and Ron was assigned to a more supportive supervisor. In addition, Ron continued to receive counseling for his attentional and learning difficulties and sought the assistance of a tutor to improve his writing skills. His job was saved, and he was able, over the course of the next several months, to clearly meet the job requirements to retain his status as an independent research scientist.

While Ron's story has a happy ending, it is important to emphasize that the process he went through to keep his job was a lengthy, emotionally exhausting one. Furthermore, he was left in the uncomfortable position of continuing to work in association with the man against whom he had defended himself in the EEOC hearings. Such proceedings should only be undertaken as a last resort, and only if there seem to be no desirable work alternatives elsewhere.

Negotiating Instead

Instead of bringing a lawsuit against your employer, you might consider negotiating the terms of your departure. Lawsuits are painful and expensive for employers as well as employees. Usually both parties would much rather avoid such an action. If you have a documented disability, feel that you have not received reasonable accommodations made in good faith, and feel that your employer is placing pressure on you to resign, it may be best to talk directly to your supervisor; discuss your grievances, your rights, and your disability; and suggest that a settlement be negotiated prior to your voluntary departure to avoid the pain and expense of a lawsuit for all concerned. In exchange for dropping the lawsuit and leaving voluntarily, you might consider negotiating for the following:

1. Employment extended for a specific time period during which you actively seek another job
2. Severance pay
3. Strong letter of recommendation

A satisfactory severance package was won by a man who was himself a lawyer. He had done very productive work for his organization over a number of years. When the administration changed, however, his ADHD traits of poor organization and poor time management were much less tolerated by the new regime. This man suspected he had ADHD and obtained a diagnosis. He chose to disclose it immediately because his job was already in jeopardy. When it became clear to both sides that they faced a nasty battle, the negotiated agreement was a relief to all. Unfortunately, most adults with ADHD don't have the leverage to negotiate such a departure.

Conclusion

To summarize, the ADA has given much-needed support in the workplace to persons with disabilities and is leading to improved awareness of and sensitivity to disabled persons at work. The law, as it is written, is broad and general. What accommodations are reasonable for a person with ADHD to request of his or her employer has not yet been established.

If things have gone so wrong that you are strongly considering a lawsuit, you should even more strongly consider alternative employment! Bringing a lawsuit against an employer is lengthy and costly. There is no guarantee that you will win the suit, and if you do, there is little likelihood that keeping the job you have fought for will be good for you. There are certainly circumstances in which filing a suit is appropriate, but in the majority of cases, the process will be painful and destructive and will take your attention away from making positive changes in your work life. Normally, it is much easier to find a better position than to force an unwilling employer to improve your current one. Don't lose sight of your real objective: finding a workplace where you can grow and thrive.

Notes

1 Americans With Disabilities Act, U.S. Code, vol. 42, sees. 12101 et seq (1990).
2 Job Accommodations Network, a service of the President's Commission on Employment of People with Disabilities, 809 Allen Hall, West Virginia University, Morgantown, WV, 26506.

IN THIS CHAPTER

This chapter discusses a range of workplace accommodations that may help improve on-the-job functioning for individuals with ADHD.

13

Strategies and Accommodations to Function Better at Work

The Americans with Disabilities Act[1] (discussed in Chapter 12) calls on employers to make reasonable accommodations for people with documented disabilities. However, what constitutes "reasonable" accommodations is not clearly defined. This chapter focuses on how you can be proactive and self-reliant rather than focusing on how your employer can accommodate you. The Job Accommodations Network (JAN)[2] lists accommodations that have been provided by employers to employees with ADHD. However, because an accommodation is listed by JAN does not guarantee that your employee must provide this accommodation. Accommodations must be "reasonable" according to the size and circumstances of your particular employer.

Consider Working with an ADHD Career Coach

One of the most important steps you might take is to look for an experienced ADHD job coach who can not only make suggestions and help you to find solutions but can also provide structure and support as you work to implement new strategies to function better at work. Managing ADHD at work is *your* responsibility, and there are many things you can to do change your work environment and improve your functioning at work. Working closely with an experienced ADHD career coach can help you identify supports you can request while also developing strategies to reduce your ADHD challenges at work.

While accommodations are clear cut in the case of disabilities such as vision or hearing impairments, appropriate accommodations for ADHD are much more complicated to identify because there is such a range of differences among those with ADHD in terms of both needs and severity of symptoms. Unlike most other disabilities, accommodations for ADHD must be custom tailored to suit:

1. your particular needs
2. the specific requirements of your job
3. the specific characteristics of your work environment

So don't try to figure it out alone, and don't assume the psychiatrist or psychologist who diagnosed you is fully informed regarding workplace accommodations. Your best bet is to seek someone with specific ADHD workplace coaching/counseling experience. While there may not be such an expert in your geographic location, this does not need to be an impediment. ADHD career coaching is typically conducted via phone or Skype. So seek the best advice and guidance, even if the person you work with is geographically distant.

Request Accommodations Informally without Disclosure of ADHD

It's often best when accommodations are requested without disclosing that you have ADHD. Employers, unfortunately, often hold a very negative view of ADHD because they are only familiar with stereotypical notions of ADHD and are not aware that many high-functioning individuals can also have ADHD. In order to avoid triggering negative assumptions, your first steps toward making your job more ADHD friendly should not involve disclosure of ADHD. Instead, always approach your boss in a problem-solving mode, stating a problem and suggesting one or more potential solutions. For instance:

> *"I've got a problem with the noise level in my office. It's hard to concentrate because my officemate is speaking loudly on the phone during most of the day. I'm wondering if I could change desks and work around people that aren't often talking on the phone."*

While your problem may be intensified because of your ADHD, you don't need to tell your employer that. He or she can readily understand why you might want a more quiet work area. If you are seen as a motivated, hard worker, your supervisor has lots of motivation to provide you with a workspace in which you can become even more productive.

What Types of Accommodations Might Be Helpful for You

In what follows, you can find a list of accommodations that have been helpful for employees with ADHD. Read through them considering whether they might be useful in your own work setting.

Accommodations in Supervisory Techniques

- Meet more frequently.
- Set short-term, concrete goals.
- Give more emphasis to positive outcomes.
- Clarify guidelines and job performance expectations.
- Provide frequent job performance reviews and use concrete, reasonable measures to assess improvement; give regular positive feedback as well.
- Evaluate employee in terms of strengths, not just weaknesses.

It's not likely that your supervisor has knowledge or experience in accommodating an adult with ADHD. Often, it can be helpful for you to work with an ADHD job coach and then work with your supervisor to help him or her better understand you and your needs. In many cases, you'll need to coach your supervisor in order for him or her to meet your needs. For example, you might explain that a brief weekly meeting to review progress and reevaluate priorities would be very helpful to you. If you can assure your supervisor that this can be a brief, efficient meeting, not time-consuming hand-holding, this request is much more likely to be met. Likewise, you can request that your supervisor send all requests and comments via e-mail rather than through verbal requests. If your supervisor feels that this will be too much work, you can request to use a software program that allows your smartphone to record all conversations, which are then translated into text. This program, called Audio Notetaker, in conjunction with the Sonocent Recorder (www.sonocent.com), allows you to quickly highlight key items in the text to pull out a clear list of tasks, comments, or requests that your supervisor has made in your meeting. In requesting accommodations, the key is to minimize additional work for your supervisor and to demonstrate a high level of motivation to do your job well and efficiently.

General Accommodations for ADHD Adults in the Workplace

Changes in Job Description

- Remove from job descriptions particular tasks that cause the most difficulty. (Note: Your employer is certainly not required to make changes in your job description, but if you function well in key aspects of the job, they may be inclined to modify your job to suit your strengths.)
- Increase proportion of tasks that are more closely suited to employees' strengths and interests.

General Accommodations for ADHD Adults in the Workplace *(continued)*

Changes in Communication Patterns

- Provide more written communications.
- Communicate more frequently.

Changes in the Physical Work Environment

- Provide a less distracting environment.
- Change lighting.
- Provide a white-noise machine to mask auditory distractions.
- Provide the assistance of a professional organizer to reduce clutter.

Use of Assistive Technologies

- Use a recorder to record ideas and reminders. There are now smartphone apps that can record meetings or conversations, turn voice into text, and allow you to edit them to create a concise outline.
- Use timers or beepers to on your smartphone to increase time awareness.
- Use voice-to-text computer software (such as Naturally Speaking) to assist with writing.

Provision of Specialized Training to Enhance Functioning

- Offer time-management seminars.
- Offer seminars teaching organizational skills.
- Pay for individual training with a job coach.

Symptom-Specific Accommodations for ADHD

Distractibility

- Change location of work space to a less distracting location.
- Permit use of meeting rooms, library, or another's private office when available.
- Permit working at home for some defined fraction of the work week.
- Permit use of flextime in order to work during the less-distracting off-peak hours.
- Use headphones to mask distracting sounds.

Symptom-Specific Accommodations for ADHD *(continued)*

- Assign officemates with compatible work styles.
- Route phone calls to voicemail to minimize interruptions.
- Provide a private office.

Hyperactivity/Need for Physical Movement

- Transfer to a job that allows more physical movement.
- Shift work hours to allow an extended exercise period at midday.
- Permit extended breaks several times a day for walking.
- Permit work in varied locations.
- Minimize need for participation in extended meetings.
- Provide a desk that can be modified for sitting or standing.
- Provide a treadmill desk to allow movement while working.

Difficulty with Organization/Planning/Follow-Through

- Provide possibility of teamwork with someone who can provide structure.
- Permit frequent face-to-face supervision.
- Establish expectation of frequent updates to supervisor—by e-mail or shared documents.
- Assistance in breaking down long-term assignments into daily tasks.
- Provide training in time management and organization.
- Provide software to assist in scheduling and planning.
- Assist in devising an ADHD–friendly filing system.
- Hire a professional organizer to organize physical office space (regular, repeated assistance is typically most useful).
- Provide training in management and supervision if these duties are part of job description.
- Provide coach to assist those with ADHD in ongoing development of better organizational skills.
- Provide checklists to give structure to multistage tasks.
- Provide regular assistance in prioritizing tasks, particularly if task assignments come from multiple sources.
- Provide sample forms, letters, and so forth to use as models.

Paperwork Problems

- Provide clerical support to handle paperwork.
- Reduce paperwork requirements.

Symptom-Specific Accommodations for ADHD *(continued)*

- Provide a coach to assist those with ADHD in developing better paperwork techniques.
- Permit exchange of job duties with other workers (e.g., exchange phone duties for filing).
- Simplify forms and paperwork requirements.

Memory Difficulties

- Follow up verbal communications in writing.
- Make written communications clear and concise.
- Use video or audio equipment to record meetings.
- Provide training in memory enhancement.
- Train ADHD employees in use of a day planner as a memory aid.
- Regularly post notices of events.
- Provide notes or minutes of meetings.

What Accommodations Is My Employer Required to Provide for Me?

If you have questions of a legal nature, refer to Chapter 12 to better understand what your employer is required to provide under the Americans with Disabilities Act.[3]

Keep in mind that as a general rule the primary responsibility for managing your ADHD remains with you. Many approaches outlined in other chapters are steps you can take without the participation of your employer. Your employer and supervisor should be engaged in the process only when you have a need that cannot be met without their permission or cooperation.

Conclusion

Don't rely on your employer to take responsibility for understanding what accommodations you might need. Be proactive. You must always take charge of your ADHD needs. Many of the accommodations described in this chapter are things you can provide for yourself or can arrange for yourself. If you must look to your employer to accommodate you, it remains your responsibility to understand your needs and present them to your employer. Make reasonable requests for accommodations that are compatible with the overall functioning of the organization.

What's good for ADHD is good for the organization. Everyone struggles with some of the symptoms associated with ADHD—absentmindedness, distractibility, disorganization, and difficulties with verbal memory and decision making. Employees with ADHD strongly need accommodations, but everyone can potentially benefit from them. Employers who become more sensitive and responsive to the needs of those with ADHD will find that in the process of improving the efficiency of their ADHD employees, they have developed approaches that improve the overall efficiency of the organization, thus creating a win-win situation.

Notes

1 Americans With Disabilities Act, U.S. Code, vol. 42, secs. 12101 et seq (1990).
2 Job Accommodations Network, a service of the President's Commission on Employment of People with Disabilities, 809 Allen Hall, West Virginia University, Morgantown, WV, 26506.
3 Americans With Disabilities Act, U.S. Code, vol. 42, secs. 12101 et seq (1990).

For some adults with ADHD, an office environment will never be their optimum workplace, no matter what accommodations may be available. This chapter describes some alternatives, such as telecommuting, self-employment, and multiple part-time jobs.

14

Alternatives to the "9 to 5"

Custom Designing Your Own Work Life

If you are one of those adults with ADHD who has always felt hemmed in, frustrated, or "asleep at the wheel" when working in an office, someone who has always dreamed of working for yourself, of starting your own business, and of getting out of the commuter lanes, then this is the chapter for you! When you work for yourself or in partnership with someone else, you have a much greater range of choices to custom design your work life. This chapter discusses a range of possible choices and also talks of ways to make your workday productive and your home office as ADHD friendly as possible.

Doing What You Love . . .

Of all the work-related choices you can make as an adult with ADHD, the most important one is to choose to do something you really love. It is a well-established fact that people with ADHD, when working on things that interest and intrigue them, don't just focus, but tend to hyperfocus. Hyperfocus is a state of complete engagement, when you are not aware of the passage of time and may not even be aware of people around you, even when they are speaking directly to you. When you're doing what you love, ADHD can actually become an advantage, so long as you have carefully built in the structure and support you need to attend to the less interesting but necessary aspects of work life. When you choose to do something that really interests you, while carefully designing your working life to optimize your energy and effectiveness, your likelihood of success is tremendously enhanced.

In her book *Making a Living Without a Job,* Barbara Winter writes of the importance of earning a living by being ourselves and by having fun at what we're doing.[1]

Another writer, Marsha Sinetar, author of *Do What You Love, the Money Will Follow,* describes patterns that sound remarkably like those of adults with ADHD,[2] although her comments are directed toward the general public. She writes that when people are bored, frustrated, or constrained by the work they do all day, they are plagued by drifting attention. By contrast, when a person is totally absorbed in a task and can bring his or her full attention to it, he or she becomes most effective. The process that Marsha Sinetar describes is one crucial to becoming an effective person with ADHD—to find what engages you, what intrigues you, and then to take advantage of your ADHD ability to hyperfocus.

Acknowledging Your Need for Stimulation and Variety

If you are considering developing your own business or perhaps pursuing a number of activities from a home-based office, don't let yourself be overly influenced by the naysayers. Adults with ADHD are often highly successful in very nontraditional ways. Doing several things at once or doing several different things in fairly rapid succession may be highly suitable for an adult with ADHD, who needs challenge, pressure, variety, and stimulation to perform optimally. Such approaches may seem foolhardy or too risky to those without ADHD.

In her book, Barbara Winter writes of a young man who was not diagnosed with ADHD but whose pattern resembles that of people with ADHD. He spoke of having lots of ideas and lots of projects. Rather than fearing and focusing on failure, this young man thought of his life like juggling. "*You get lots of plates spinning. If one of them crashes, you just go on to the next one. Not all of your ideas are going to work, and even your best ideas may not last. But that isn't the measure of success.*"[3] This young man recognized his need for change, stimulation, and risk taking and did not consider himself a failure if not all his attempts met with success or developed into long-term enterprises.

Thom Hartmann, a multitalented entrepreneur with ADHD, wrote of planning—actually expecting and accommodating his need to move on to new projects.[4] He, like many adults with ADHD, loved to be creative and innovative. He conceived of new projects and new products and found great excitement in bringing his ideas into reality. After this highly stimulating and creative phase, Thom knew he would lose interest and motivation. Rather than seeing this as a negative, he planned for bringing in someone with different skills and interests to take over the day-to-day management of his enterprises once he got them off the ground. Thom described himself and similar adults with ADHD as "hunters" living in a world of "farmers"—adults who can function in work that is slow, predictable, and repetitive. While ADHD hunters crave stimulation, challenge, and risk, farmers desire stability with minimal risk or challenge.

As an adult with ADHD, you should understand your differences and take them seriously. Thom Hartmann warned ADHD adults, or "hunters," not to allow the farmers of the world to set the standards by which they judge themselves. The distractibility and inability of those with ADHD to function at their best increases when they are required to do dull, unsatisfying work. However, their ability to hyperfocus, to live in the moment, and to become totally involved in a project is greater than that of the farmers. Often, by working for themselves, ADHD adults have the freedom to choose work that will turn their ADHD energy and hyperfocusing ability into a great gift.

What Goes into Creating Your Ideal Job?

While everyone with ADHD is not alike, the ideal work conditions for many adults with ADHD can be characterized by:

- An activity of high interest to you
- An optimal degree of pressure—the "Goldilocks" guidelines—not too much or you'll shut down from stress; not too little or you'll shut down from boredom—but just right—so you stay focused and on task
- Relative autonomy
- Partnership with others that have strengths in your areas of relative weakness
- Adequate structure and support—provided by either a partner or administrative assistant
- Flexibility in tasks and timetables
- An option to move on to new projects as interest wanes
- A minimum of administrative responsibilities

Why 9-to-5 Might Not Work for All Adults with ADHD

When most of us think of work, we tend to think of a standard, 9-to-5 job in an office environment, working as an employee. By definition, when we are employees, it is the employer who sets the agenda, the priorities, and the schedule. Some adults with ADHD, however, find they crave a much greater degree of flexibility and choice than can be found in the 9-to-5 world. An office environment may not be very ADHD friendly for a number of reasons:

- 9 to 5 may not be your optimal work hours.
- An open office environment may be too distracting.
- An office job may involve too much paperwork.
- Desk work may not allow enough physical movement.
- The job may involve too much work that is uninteresting, repetitive, and overly detailed.
- The job may involve long-term projects in which an adult with ADHD may lose interest long before they are finished.
- Office politics may prove frustrating and difficult.
- Corporate culture or management style may be a mismatch.

Looking at Alternatives to a 9-to-5 Existence

For individuals with ADHD, one of the great advantages of reaching adulthood is that your range of choices expands. In high school, you perhaps had very few alternatives. If you went to college, you most likely found a wider range of choices. The range of choice often becomes greater still once you enter the world of work. There are many alternatives to a 9-to-5 job. Some of those alternatives include:

- Telecommuting part time or full time
- Home-based business
- Independent professional practice
- Multiple part-time jobs
- Independent artistic or creative activities
- Entrepreneurial activities
- Consulting

Matching Alternative Solutions to Problems

If you are unhappy in your current work environment and would like to make a change, you should carefully consider which aspects of the office environment are ADHD unfriendly for you and then consider possible solutions. These solutions could range from keeping your current job while telecommuting from home on a part-time basis to having a part-time job that allows you time to develop other income-producing activities or taking the plunge and working for yourself full time.

Each of the alternatives listed in the previous section entails pluses and minuses for adults with ADHD. So in order to make a good alternative work choice:

1. Carefully consider the pros and cons of each alternative.
2. Make a realistic self-assessment, asking yourself:
   - Under what work conditions am I happiest?
   - What is most likely to make me productive and effective?
   - What are my likely downfalls?
3. Problem solve to minimize or avoid any downfalls.

Telecommuting

More and more companies are opting for telecommuting, but not everyone is well suited to telecommuting. The ideal telecommuter is:

- Output oriented
- Self-disciplined
- Trusted by managers
- Well organized
- Able to manage time well
- Self-aware and knows his or her own needs

- Able to seek help when appropriate
- Content with little interaction with coworkers, gaining more satisfaction from the work itself
- Seeking a better balance between home and work life

At first glance, this list may seem to rule out adults with ADHD as telecommuters! Self-disciplined, well organized, and good time managers? These are often pitfalls, not strengths, for ADHDers. But don't immediately discount the idea. To decide whether working from home on a part-time basis might be constructive for you, take a look at some of the pluses and minuses from an ADHD perspective.

Pluses of Telecommuting

Elimination of office distractions

The possibility of taking breaks when needed

Working time-shifted hours when preferable—telecommuting is often good for ADHD night owls

The opportunity to exercise during the day to reduce fidgetiness and restlessness

A chance to be more available to children and spouse during afternoon and early evening

Elimination of time wasted by commuting

The opportunity to dress casually and comfortably

Minuses of Telecommuting

The distractions of home: television, the Internet, projects around the house, other activities

Less structure or guidance on what to do or when to do it

No external cues to remain on task, organized, and focused

The tendency to sleep late or to procrastinate without the structure of a workplace environment

Minuses of Telecommuting *(continued)*

Loneliness, isolation

Interruptions by family

If you would like to consider telecommuting, you need to be honest in your self-evaluation and make efforts to reduce or eliminate the "minuses."

Some ways to stay on track as an ADHD telecommuter include:

1. Develop rituals and structured times to work.
2. Create an office environment at home that cues you to focus on work rather than on personal activities.
3. Check in by phone at the office when you sit down at your desk—this cues both you and your work colleagues that you are "at work."
4. Verbalize deadlines to coworkers.
5. Program a series of alarms on your smartphone throughout the day to provide structure and remind you of what you should attend to.
6. Have a regular e-mail communication at day's end with your supervisor to update him or her on your day's accomplishments.
7. Set daily goals.

Telecommuting schedules can vary widely. Some telecommuters do the great majority of their work at home and may only go to the office for specific meetings with colleagues or supervisors. Other telecommuters, like Angela, whose story is described in what follows, chose telecommuting as a part-time option best suited for work activities that required extended concentration.

Angela: A Part-Time Telecommuter

Angela worked for a small nonprofit organization. It was Angela's job to develop themes for conferences held by her

Angela: A Part-Time Telecommuter *(continued)*

organization and to oversee the planning and coordination of those conferences. Her work involved travel as well as a great deal of writing. The variety and stimulation of her work were a great match for her ADHD, but she had enormous difficulty concentrating in close quarters at the office. As she tried to write, telephones were ringing on adjacent desks, and coworkers frequently interrupted her to ask questions or to make comments.

Angela was able to negotiate with her boss to become a part-time telecommuter. She set up an organized office space at home, including computer, e-mail, telephone, and fax. She made a regular time schedule in her home office to work on those things that required sustained concentration and made herself available by phone, e-mail, and fax for ready interface with her colleagues. This arrangement provided a good solution for her distractibility while still allowing communication with her colleagues.

Operating a Home-Based Business

While a home-based business creates many of the ADHD challenges of telecommuting, it includes additional challenges that telecommuters do not have to face. Telecommuters still have ties to an employer who can provide some degree of support and structure. They also are in touch with colleagues, have tasks and deadlines set by others, must meet expectations set by others, and usually have the benefit of support staff and equipment at the office. A telecommuter coordinates her or his work with others. These connections and accountability make it easier to stay on task.

When you operate a home-based business, you have less support and structure and few, if any, connections with coworkers. Instead, you have an operation that involves a broad range of activities and responsibilities and that requires a much greater degree of independence. It is you who sets the goal, the agenda, the structure, and the pace. Let's look at Mary's story and why she encountered difficulties in her home-based business.

Mary: The Avon Lady

Mary was married and had three children. She had sold Avon products on a part-time basis for several years and decided to try her hand at developing a full-time home-based Avon business.

Mary, like many adults with ADHD, was a night owl who greatly resisted getting up in the mornings. When she had worked outside the home, she'd had no choice but to get up. As an Avon lady, she found herself sleeping later. As a result, mornings in her household became chaotic. She stayed in her pajamas, rushing her children to get dressed, fed, and out the door, and then sometimes went back to bed if she'd been up until 2 or 3 a.m. the night before.

Even when she didn't go back to bed, Mary found that she spent the first couple hours each morning drinking coffee, reading through the paper, and watching the morning television shows. She reasoned that calling people before 10 a.m. was too early. What Mary didn't do was use these hours to do household chores, work-related paperwork, or planning.

Her house did not afford her the luxury of a separate office space. She used a small desk in the kitchen to make phone calls and record orders. This desk was usually piled high, and papers often became mixed with the day's mail and the children's school papers. Her dining room became the storage area and staging ground for bagging individual Avon orders.

Mary found that she loved the social aspect of house calls and phone calls but typically spent more time socializing than selling. Orders often had to be delivered in the evenings, since many of her clients were employed full time. As a result, her evenings became more confused—in addition to dinner preparation and homework, she was now making Avon deliveries at a time when her family commitments were at their highest.

Three years later, after many battles with her husband over financial difficulties and chaos at home, Mary reluctantly

Mary: The Avon Lady *(continued)*

agreed to return to her former job as a receptionist. Mary loved the freedom, flexibility, and sociability of being a full-time Avon lady but reluctantly came to realize that she had not developed disciplined patterns that would allow her to be successful in this kind of endeavor. She finally concluded that the schedule and structure of an office job were necessary for her to stay focused.

Although a home-based business did not work for Mary, this does not mean it cannot work for you. Home-based businesses seem to work best for people with ADHD when:

1. They work with someone else. This can be a spouse, a partner, or even an employee. Interfacing with others to keep the business running provides a degree of focus and structure.
2. They have a separate area of the home from which to run their business. This area can be a basement, a garage that has been converted to an office, or even a spare bedroom.
3. They establish a routine. This routine does not have to be a "standard" daytime schedule but needs to be a disciplined routine that is not subject to procrastination or the constant invasion of personal or family activities.
4. They hire someone or work in partnership with someone who can handle the parts of the business that are most difficult for them. This typically includes paperwork, billing, filing, and record keeping.
5. They focus on their strengths—often in the area of sales, marketing, creative innovations, and product development.
6. They make sure they schedule structured time to meet their family responsibilities.

Independent Professional Practice

Professionals with ADHD often find that they are more content to work for themselves than in large practices or organizations. Whether doctors, lawyers, psychologists, financial advisors, or in other professions, professionals with ADHD typically prefer the autonomy and simplicity of a small or independent practice. Let's look at three scenarios.

Alan: (Mis)Managing a Medical Practice

Alan was an internist with never-formally-diagnosed ADHD. In the process of his daughter's evaluation for ADHD, his wife immediately recognized very strong ADHD traits in her husband. Although he was in the range of superior intelligence, he had always been highly scattered and disorganized. Alan, however, was unwilling to consider the possibility that he, too, had ADHD. Alan's denial of ADHD became the "last straw" in an already heavy burden borne by his wife.

Concluding that he had no intention of looking at himself and trying to change destructive patterns, his wife decided to leave the marriage. In the process of the separation, she also resigned from serving as his office manager. For years she had kept his schedule, reminded him of deadlines and events, and nagged him to keep up with paperwork and dictation. Despite all her efforts, however, the office was a shambles. He typically came home with a foot-high pile of charts, resolving to catch upon his dictations, only to fall asleep in front of the television.

Following the separation, Alan's practice further deteriorated very rapidly. Overwhelmed by the organizational tasks of running an independent private practice and unable to find someone to take over all the tasks his wife had juggled, he sold his practice and took position within a large managed-care organization, where most of the administrative tasks were managed by others.

Scott: From Teacher to Real Estate Agent

Scott was a highly gifted teacher whose ADHD helped him be dynamic and creative in the classroom. Grading papers and record keeping, however, had always been a tremendous struggle. He and his wife, a fellow teacher, wanted to have children and concluded that two teachers' salaries could not comfortably support a family. Scott felt that his personable, high-energy nature would be a good match for real-estate sales. His father-in-law invited him to join the real estate firm where he had worked for many years.

One year later, however, Scott sought counseling. He felt anxious, depressed, and very disturbed with his lack of success as a real estate agent. He described his days as drifting and unfocused. After his wife left each morning for her teaching job, he found himself procrastinating, watching television, going to the local gym, walking the dog—almost anything except drumming up business. He disliked making cold calls and detested the detailed paperwork.

Through counseling, Scott recognized that the isolation and complete lack of structure of his day were paralyzing for him. He resolved to schedule time each day at the real estate office, manning the phones, making contacts with potential clients, and learning ways to build his client base from fellow agents. Scott also decided to apprentice himself to another agent, accompanying him on calls with clients. Scott learned through his counseling and the positive results from the changes he made that he needed the support provided by mentoring and the structure provided by regular hours spent in the office.

Barry: Independent Financial Consultant

Barry had arranged a professional life for himself in which he found both personal satisfaction and financial success. Let's look carefully at his approach and how it differed from Alan's

Barry: Independent Financial Consultant *(continued)*

and Scott's. In studying these differences, you may find some clues to structuring a successful professional practice for yourself as an adult with ADHD.

Barry was a highly independent financial consultant whose consulting practice thrived. What did he do differently from Scott and Alan? Primarily, Barry was able to see himself realistically, with detachment and accuracy, and to make changes in his work life accordingly.

Early in his career, he had worked in a large brokerage firm, a position he found constraining. In his mid-thirties, he decided to take the plunge and open his own private office. Realistic about his strengths, he knew that he excelled at developing a client base, inspiring confidence in clients, and making strong recommendations for investment opportunities. Equally realistic about his ADHD traits, he recognized the need to establish order, flexibility, and low stress in his work environment. He rented office space a scant ten minutes from his home. Knowing his weakness in the areas of paperwork and record keeping, he wisely convinced his administrative assistant in the large firm to move with him to his private firm. She already had an in-depth knowledge of the business and of record-keeping needs and procedures.

Barry created a work environment in which he was in charge, which gave him the flexibility to take breaks during the day when they were needed and to keep his workflow at a manageable level. He was also realistic about the amount of work required to run an independent consulting firm. He worked very hard, but on a schedule that suited his own bio-rhythms. He taught his administrative assistant to protect him from unnecessary interruptions and to handle as much of the administrative work as possible without involving him.

Barry's business was soon thriving. Although he could have easily expanded by taking on associates and creating a

Barry: Independent Financial Consultant *(continued)*

bustling financial advising service, he was smart enough to realize that he didn't want to recreate an environment similar to that which he had voluntarily left a number of years earlier. After fifteen years of independent work, he had created the ideal life for himself, earning a comfortable living, keeping his stress level low, and recognizing his limitations as well as his strengths.

Multiple Part-Time Jobs

Having two or more part-time jobs can sometimes be an ideal solution for an adult with ADHD. If you're working for others in these part-time jobs, the structure and time lines are built-in. By having more than one job, there is more movement and variety, which helps prevent the boredom and restlessness that so often plague adults with ADHD in the workplace.

Wayne: Have Social Work Degree, Will Travel

Wayne was a clinical social worker with ADHD who arranged a work schedule that kept him interested and active. Initially, after earning his degree, he found a full-time job in a social service agency. There he found that the work was repetitive and the work load was stressful. A great percentage of his time was taken up with paperwork. All of these are warning signals for adults with ADHD. After a couple years, Wayne felt very dissatisfied and began to search for work alternatives.

Changes in his work life evolved gradually. At first, he accepted part-time work in the evening in an agency that dealt with the elderly. There he co-led a counseling group for people in retirement homes. He found he enjoyed the interpersonal interaction as well as the very low demand for paperwork. He was well

Wayne: Have Social Work Degree, Will Travel *(continued)*

liked and was offered more work over the next several months. Through his professional grapevine, he learned of part-time work of a similar nature at a large private agency that dealt with the needs of the elderly.

Over the course of a year, Wayne resigned from his full-time job, having been able to arrange two part-time jobs offering him equal pay and greater satisfaction. Because he was not a member of the full-time staff of either agency, his presence was normally not required at administrative meetings, allowing him to focus on the clinical work that he loved. He enjoyed the variety of going to different work sites on different days, the reduced paperwork requirements, and the stimulation of a variety of professional activities.

Anne: Two Part-Time Jobs, Two Careers

Anne was a trained nurse who loved working with and helping people, but she was very unhappy in the managed health care environment where she was employed. A highly trained, intelligent woman, she found that the stress and lack of autonomy in her work life were having a very negative effect on her attitude and professional satisfaction.

Anne entered ADHD career-focused counseling. She and her counselor engaged in creative problem solving. Anne decided to take a risk and give up her frustrating but highly secure job in order to seek greater personal satisfaction. She was hired as a part-time clinical supervisor to younger, less-experienced visiting nurses in the community. Anne loved the opportunity to pass on her knowledge as well as the recognition and respect she gained as an instructor and supervisor.

Anne: Two Part-Time Jobs, Two Careers *(continued)*

At the same time, she found an outlet for her love of writing, something she had pursued in college but had found no time for when employed as a full-time nurse. She was hired half time to work on a nursing newsletter, editing and writing articles. This gave her a much-desired intellectual outlet and the opportunity to become a thought leader in the nursing profession, writing about ways in which she felt her profession needed to change.

Anne had exchanged an inflexible full-time job for two very different part-time jobs, both of which offered her intellectual stimulation and challenge. In both of these positions, she had not only structure and interaction but also a high degree of autonomy and variety—often an ideal combination for an adult with ADHD.

Creative Activities at Home

Have you ever dreamed of writing the great American novel, of developing the artistic talent you've ignored for years, of advancing your skills as a potter, weaver, or other type of craftsperson? For some adults with ADHD, the urge to create and the satisfaction of creative activity are among their strongest driving forces.

The pros and cons are very similar to any type of work that you might pursue at home on a completely independent basis: how to keep yourself focused and how to meet your needs for structure, administrative support, and social contact without detracting from your work at home. And, of course, how to earn enough money to support your needs.

Larry: An ADHD Photographer

Larry was a highly talented photographer whose home-based photography business fell apart when his wife, Lynn, grew tired of dedicating her life to keeping her ADHD husband focused. For a

Larry: An ADHD Photographer *(continued)*

number of years, she had been his business manager, taking care of advertising, marketing and billing and serving as his agent in setting up photography exhibits. He became well known in his community for his intuitive, highly personal portraits as well as for more abstract, artistic photography. When Lynn gave up being his support system, Larry's business rapidly faltered. Unlike Barry, the financial consultant, he had no experience in establishing supports for himself. He had married his support system, and his support system had resigned.

Through counseling with the couple, Lynn agreed to return to working with him on a limited-time basis and to helping him "grow up" professionally by finding and hiring the necessary supports to replace her. During the course of the next year, Larry found a photography assistant who also had good organizational skills. He also located an agent to promote his gallery work. Eventually, with his assistant's and agent's support, Larry's business thrived once again. He developed a line of note cards featuring his photographs and found a publisher to print a calendar of scenes he had photographed of the local Pennsylvania countryside. Two years after Lynn's final resignation, Larry found that he had, in fact, been able to build a professional support system that functioned even better than his wife had. And even better, his marriage improved once his wife could pursue her own work and not dedicate herself to propping up her husband's career.

Michael: Novelist or Internet Addict?

Michael was an adult with ADHD who worked as a technical writer in the computer industry. He enjoyed the opportunity for travel that his work afforded him and worked well under the pressure of publishing deadlines. Michael, however, had always dreamed of writing fiction. An English major in college, he had pursued work

Michael: Novelist or Internet Addict? *(continued)*

as a technical writer as a practical move after graduation. When his industry newsletter was bought by a larger newsletter, Michael's job was eliminated. Rather than looking for another position, Michael and his wife, Anne, decided to see this turn of events as an opportunity for him to pursue his dream. Anne's recent promotion allowed them more financial flexibility. They decided Michael would stay home and work on his novel, which had been gathering dust in the corner since he'd abandoned work on it years earlier.

One year later, however, Michael felt anxious and depressed. With medication and with the structure of deadlines and short-term projects, he had functioned well. Now, at home full time, with no structure, no social contact, and no deadlines, Michael found himself sleeping late, struggling with writer's block, and spending more and more of his time writing e-mail messages to other lonely people. He was hungry for personal contact, and his social world consisted of interactions with others he had "met" online.

Through counseling, Michael recognized that having all the time in the world to write was not an advantage for him. Rather than give up his dream of completing his novel, he decided to do two things to give more structure to his day. First, he contacted former colleagues in the technical writing field and found a part-time job. This job got him up in the morning, gave him some social contact, and lent structure to his workweek. Second, he joined a writer's group. In this group, each writer brought ongoing work to share and critique. This way, he found that he kept more focused when writing. He had only a limited number of hours each week in which to write, and he had a group that was expecting to hear about his progress on a weekly basis. Understanding his need for structure, support, and accountability to others, Michael finally found a work–life combination that allowed him to be focused and productive in pursuing his dream of fiction writing.

Consulting

For many adults with ADHD, the life of a consultant may provide the best of both worlds: the more structured world of the corporate office environment and the flexible world of the self-employed. When you are a consultant, it's easier to work outside arbitrary rules and rigid people. If you don't enjoy consulting with a particular company, you can always move on to one you enjoy working with more. At the same time, consulting does not involve the investment and risk of entrepreneurial ventures. Unlike an entrepreneur who is developing new services or products, a consultant is working with a familiar set of skills he or she has already developed and is often working with people with whom he or she already has a long-established relationship. For these reasons, there is more familiarity and more built-in structure. Consultants can command high hourly wages as experts in their field without having to struggle with the non–ADHD-friendly responsibilities of managing people within a large firm.

As with all of the variants of more independent work life that have been discussed in this chapter, the downside of consulting is often related to administrative details. Many adults with ADHD describe that the consulting work itself is very satisfying. They find that generating ideas and verbal communication are easy for them. However, the necessary follow-up reports, record keeping, and billing can be their downfall.

Tools for Success in Self-Created Jobs

In the first section of this chapter a variety, of alternatives to a 9-to-5 job have been explored, considering the pros and cons of each alternative. No matter which alternative you might be considering, there are a number of patterns, techniques, or approaches that may make your efforts to custom design your work life more likely to succeed.

Create Your Own Support Network

If you choose to work independently, one of the most effective ways to combat the negative effects of your ADHD is to create a team or support network around you. Who is part of this network and how elaborate it is depends on your needs and activities.

Support staff. Many consultants, home-based businesspeople, or professionals starting out in independent practice protest that they cannot afford support staff. If you have ADHD, the reality is more likely that you can't afford *not to* have support. This doesn't mean you must hire a full-time assistant. There are many creative ways to meet your needs without overextending yourself financially. Many people with professional secretarial skills have their own home-based business and can work for you on an hourly basis doing all kinds of administrative work—typing, record keeping, billing, tax reports, and so on. They don't even need to come to your office. With the convenience of answering machines, fax machines, and e-mail, it is quite possible to stay in close touch without being physically in the same environment.

Partnerships. Another way to create a support network is to form a partnership. Some adults with ADHD find that having a partner or partners in their enterprises helps keep them on track and gives them a forum for processing new ideas as well as a way to divide work according to the skills and preferences of the partners. Even less formally, it is possible to work in partnership with one or more people on specific projects without forming a legal partnership.

Support groups for the self-employed. Many self-employed individuals who work out of their homes, whether they have ADHD or not, feel isolated and hungry for interaction with others. Finding or forming a group of fellow self-employed professionals can play a very important role in the life of a self-employed individual. A group affords them social stimulation of a professional nature and allows them to share experiences, problems, and solutions. In the process, some of these professionals have formed contacts with one another that can enhance their work projects.

You may find that some or all of these approaches for forming a support network are helpful to you in developing and maintaining your independent work life. What seems clear, however, is that most adults with ADHD seem to function better when they have the opportunity to get feedback, share ideas, build structure, and delegate non–ADHD-friendly tasks to employees, contractors, or partners.

Tools for Managing Your Time and Work at Home

Self-awareness and honest self-assessment are crucial if you are going to be successful in working at home, creating your own structure for managing your time.

Recognize Your Hours of Peak Productivity

The more independently you work, the more important good time-management skills become. This doesn't mean inflexibility, but it does mean discipline. Know yourself and your peak performance hours, and schedule your at-home work accordingly.

Know Your Limits of Sustained Concentration

Depending on your areas of strength and weakness, you'll be able to perform some tasks with greater prolonged concentration than others. Don't make plans that require you to go beyond reasonable limits. Observe yourself and experiment to learn not only the best times of day but also the best lengths of time you should devote to certain activities. A good rule of thumb is that the more difficult the task, the shorter the time period that should be allocated to the task in a stretch. Move to a completely different activity and then come back to your more challenging task when your energy level is stronger.

Plan Your Day—Don't Just Respond to Your Day as It Unfolds

You should make a plan for each day, either at the end of the previous workday or as you begin your new workday. And don't confuse planning with scheduling.

Planning is what you are going to do. Scheduling is when you are going to do it.

After you have made your plan for the day, schedule when and in what order you are going to carry out your plan. A plan doesn't have to be inflexible. If circumstances change, don't give up your plan; rather, alter your plan according to the unforeseen events, and then proceed with the altered plan.

To-Do Lists

Make your to-do lists work for you, but don't become a slave to them. Some adults with ADHD make daily task lists that are overwhelming and unrealistic. Creating a to-do list that is unrealistic only creates overwhelming feelings and a sense that you've gotten little accomplished. A right-sized to-do list is one you regularly complete by day's end.

Keep both a master to-do list and a daily to-do list. Your master list contains all of the to-dos that you can possibly think of, grouped by category or project. As you think of things or conceive of new projects, those to-dos go on your master list. Your daily to-do list is the list you intend and expect to complete by day's end. Don't put a major task on a daily to-do list unless it can realistically be completed from start to finish on that day. Instead, define a specific aspect of the larger task—one that has a beginning and an end—and put that on your daily to-do list. Tasks should move fluidly from your master list to your daily list—the master list is a storage system. Your daily list only contains that day's action items.

Don't play games with your to-do lists. Some people feel so gratified by checking items off their list that they only focus on the easy-to-accomplish tasks, rewarding themselves with more check marks while avoiding the more important, more challenging tasks of the day.

To make the most of a daily to-do list:

1. Write a realistic, doable list.
2. Take care of items on that list in order of importance.
3. Take advantage of odd moments that might otherwise be wasted to take care of the quick and easy to-do items rather than beginning your day with them.

Make Your Moods Work *for* You

Many adults with ADHD report that they can only work when they are "in the mood." That may sound almost childish, but if you can catch the mood for doing a particular task, you're likely to be much more productive. This doesn't mean you should your moods as a reason to avoid work, but rather to "catch the wave" if you are in the mood to do one important task rather than another.

If you find that you are never "in the mood" for an important task, you'll need to do some problem solving to understand what's in the way. Use your moods as a powerful engine that can drive great productivity. Shift from task to task as your mood and energy level change. When you work at home, you have much greater flexibility. Write during your peak hours, then do more mundane tasks as your energy level falls. Schedule necessary meetings or business-related errands for times when you feel restless or energy depleted.

Getting Past Procrastination

Procrastination is often a struggle for adults with ADHD, even in a structured office environment. The possibilities for procrastination multiply with a home-based workplace, where little or no external structure is provided and there are few, if any, people to report to. If you tend to be a procrastinator, you need to work even harder to develop antiprocrastination tools, particularly if you are considering working at home. Here are some approaches that can help:

1. Do the unpleasant stuff first. For many, filing is one of those tasks that gets put off. They find that if they leave it to the end of their workday, they're likely to tell themselves, "I'm tired. I'll do it tomorrow." But by starting your day with filing, you can create order so you can work more efficiently for the remainder of the day.
2. Break unpleasant tasks into tolerable "bites." If you have a huge task facing you that you dread, break it into ten-minute segments. Do ten minutes of the task each morning and another ten each afternoon. Sometimes you'll find that once you've overcome your inertia about the task, you may go beyond your ten-minute commitment. Then you'll have outsmarted your procrastination!
3. Set a deadline and make it known to others. Make verbal commitments to others. Saying "I'll fax that report to you by the end of the day" makes it more likely to happen.

4. Promise yourself a reward. Give yourself something to look forward to. Tell yourself, "I'll take a walk, call a friend, or get a snack, after I've written that letter." Be sure to make the reward immediate. It will motivate you more.

5. Delegate. There may be tasks so burdensome to you that it is much smarter to delegate that task to someone else. In a home-based business, this usually means hiring an assistant or specialist. You may protest, "But I can't afford that expense!" In some instances, you can't afford not to.

Tips for Making Your Independent Workday Productive

Get an Early Start

"As your first hour goes, so goes the rest of the day!" Remember, it's the early bird who catches the worm. Don't give in to the temptation to sleep in, read the paper for an hour, or otherwise put off starting your workday just because you don't have a boss looking over your shoulder. You'll most likely find you are more productive if you take breaks later in the day when your concentration wanes rather than "goofing off" at the beginning.

If You Start Your Day With E-mail, You're Inviting the World to Create Your Daily To-Do List!

While you may need to quickly scan your e-mail to make sure that there is no critical message awaiting you, don't make clearing out your e-mail the first task of the day. Why not? Because going to your e-mail is a default task—it's there waiting for you—and by reading through your e-mail is basically inviting the world to hijack the plans for your day. Instead, start your day with your most critical task, then check your e-mail as a break from work that requires more intense concentration or effort.

Begin (or End) Your Day with a Planning Session

The most important fifteen minutes of your day should be spent planning, prioritizing, and scheduling your day. During this daily planning session, review your daily task list, and schedule when you plan to accomplish each task (or cluster of tasks). Use this time for longer-term planning as well. Don't let the mundane to-dos take up all your time, while you never seem to have time for more challenging tasks such as creating a business plan, doing marketing to grow your business, or writing a report or letter that is due.

Build in Check-In Times with Someone Else

Normally this check-in would be with a colleague, supervisor (if you are a telecommuter), or partner. If you are completely solo in your work, this check-in can be with an ADHD coach, an assistant, or your spouse. These check-ins should help you keep on track. Talk about what you plan to accomplish that day or what you have accomplished.

Identify Personal Temptations and Distractions

Identify your personal temptations. These might include television watching, reading the paper, talking on the phone, playing computer games, or going online to interact with others. Then problem solve to figure out ways to make these distractions less available.

Develop solutions to limit these temptations. Make a rigid rule: no TV during your specified work hours. Alternatively, use these temptations as rewards for completing work-related tasks that are unappealing to you.

Set Boundaries for Yourself between Personal and Work Life at Home

One of the advantages of working for yourself or working at home is that you can more conveniently take care of personal and family business during the week. Make sure this advantage doesn't become a pitfall, however, by consistently robbing you of time you intended to devote to your work. It may help to schedule personal time: For example, set aside designated parts of your day or parts of your week for appointments, grocery shopping, chores, and the like.

If you have the necessary time awareness and self-discipline, you may choose to move back and forth between professional activities and personal activities throughout your day, choosing to exercise, work in the garden, or prepare a meal as a break from your work activities when you find that your concentration is waning. The key here is to manage those breaks so that an intended half-hour break doesn't grow into extended, unintended time away from your work.

Set Boundaries for Your Family between Work and Personal Life

It is important for your spouse and children to realize that just because you're home doesn't mean you're not "at work." Your spouse may assume that you are the obvious choice for running errands during the day since he or she is at work and you are at home. Your spouse or other family members are less likely to respect work/personal life boundaries if you don't respect them. If you are prone to watch TV or surf the Internet in the afternoon when you intended to be working, you are certainly inviting your spouse or children to request that you pick up the dry cleaning, run to the store, or drive the carpool!

The issues for young children who have a working parent at home should also be addressed. It is difficult for young children to understand and accept that even though their mother or father is at home, they cannot be disturbed or spoken to because they are working. If you have young children at home, unexpected interruptions are inevitable. However, the separation of work and family life becomes easier for children to understand as they become older.

It is helpful if your at-home work space is completely separate from your family's living space so that psychologically you are at work rather than at home. Of course, you will blur those boundaries if your children see you wandering into the kitchen for a drink or a snack at odd moments! Many parents who work at home find that their productive work hours are when their children are at school or asleep at night.

Creating an ADHD–Friendly Work Space at Home

Having a Dedicated Work Space Helps You Dedicate Yourself to Work!

If possible, have an office space at home that is not used for other purposes by other family members. One of the huge advantages of working independently at home as a telecommuter or working for yourself is that you have the opportunity to create an ADHD–friendly work space for yourself. Some may have the good fortune to have a very private, separate work space at home, while others may have to creatively devise this space. Be careful, however, not to shortchange yourself. You will need a separate, closed-off space dedicated to your work and organized to suit your work, even if it means giving up a dining room or guest room to create an office. This dedicated space is essential to reduce distractions and to help keep you focused and organized. Using a space dedicated to work helps to give you an "at work" mindset you aren't likely to have sitting at the kitchen table.

Turn Off Your Cell Phone During Times You Need to Concentrate

Check voice-mail messages and return calls in blocks of time rather than allowing others to randomly interrupt your workday and break your concentration. If partners or family members need to have direct, immediate contact with you, have a dedicated phone line that only they have access to. Others should call you on your work cell number, leaving you a message to return at your convenience.

Consider leaving a message on your voicemail explaining that you are available for direct calls during specific hours.

A Clear Desk Leads to Clear Thinking!

A clear desk greatly enhances your ability to focus and to sustain your concentration. In fact, serene, uncluttered surroundings in your entire work space will enhance your effectiveness. Even if you are not successful in keeping up with your filing, try to arrange your office space so your piles are not on your desk and are not in your immediate line of vision as you work. Some people find that a credenza placed to the side—or, better yet, behind their desk chair—can serve this purpose. On the credenza (or shelf) you can place baskets for action items, such as items to file, or items to mail, leaving your desk clear except for the materials you are currently using.

If You Can't Easily *Use* Your Filing System, You Don't *Have* One!

Many adults with ADHD working at home find that developing and maintaining a filing system is one of the most difficult tasks they face. Many develop a very detailed filing system, which they don't use consistently because it is too labor intensive to maintain. Some adults with ADHD report that they have created duplicate files with slightly differing names because they have not developed a simple, logical filing system. Remember, if you don't use your filing system, you don't have a filing system!

While everyone must develop a system that works for them, a general guideline to keeping up with your filing is to make your system as simple as possible. It is far better to have a few large files than to have detailed files that are underused as unfiled papers pile up on every horizontal surface in your office. One man with ADHD developed an almost primitive filing system that worked well for him. He purchased a series of square plastic containers, the type sold in discount stores for storing toys, clothing, and the like. He wrote a large label on each, which pertained to some large project or some large aspect of his work, and then literally tossed papers into these storage containers that were lined up on a shelf across one wall of his office. He might have had to do a little searching within each basket to find a particular document, but at least he had created a system simple enough to guarantee that the paper would be somewhere in that particular pile rather than mixed together with unrelated papers.

A Pleasant, Soothing Work Environment Enhances Productivity

Create a pleasant, soothing, but nondistracting work space. While most of us have little control over our work environment when we are employed by someone else, we have many more degrees of latitude when we create a work space for ourselves at home. It is important to put some thought into arranging your work space to best meet your needs. Many individuals find that they work better when they are exposed to natural sunlight. Place your desk near a window. If you are prone to distract yourself by looking out the window, place your chair facing away from the window but still near it to enjoy the benefit of sunlight.

Don't Allow Physical Discomfort to Distract You

Invest in a comfortable chair. You'll be spending a considerable amount of time sitting in it. Make sure, if you write at a computer, that your keyboard is at keyboard height and not desk height. Spending hours holding your hands and arms several inches too high can lead to muscle tension and neck and shoulder problems.

In general, the more ADHD friendly your work space is, the more productive you are likely to be.

Conclusion

By working independently, whether as telecommuters, consultants, artists, or businesspersons, adults with ADHD have the greatest opportunity to custom design their work life. First, try to make an accurate self-assessment. In the numerous ADHD stories contained in this chapter, some individuals were very successful in choosing a line of work they loved and in setting up a work environment in which they could function well; others found themselves barely able to function when they were completely on their own. If you are working at home, but struggling with disorganization and procrastination, you may be able to make good use of some of the techniques suggested in this chapter for getting and staying on track. After an honest self-examination, you may decide that, like it or not, you function better as an employee in a more structured job. The important thing is to find the levels of stimulation, variety, and autonomy that work best for you.

Notes

1 Winter, Barbara. (2010). *Making a Living Without a Job, revised edition: Winning Ways for Creating Work that you Love*. New York, NY: Random House, LLC.

2 Sinetar, Marsha. (2015). *Do What you Love, the Money will Follow: Discover Your Right Livelihood.* Santa Rosa, CA: Sinetar and Associates.

3 Winter, Barbara. (2010). *Making a Living Without a Job, revised edition: Winning Ways for Creating Work that you Love*. New York, NY: Random House, LLC.

4 Hartmann, T. (1993). *Attention Deficit Disorder: A Different Perception.* Penn Valley, CA: Underwood.

IN THIS CHAPTER

This chapter discusses general issues for women with ADHD as well as the impact some of those issues have on their functioning in the workplace.

15

Workplace Issues for Women with ADHD

In recent years, it has become clear that women are affected by ADHD in numbers almost equal to those of men. While many of the struggles are the same for men and women—problems with time management, organization, planning, procrastination, and forgetfulness—men and women with ADHD are also affected by biological, social, and cultural differences. In this chapter, I'll highlight some of the most critical differences and how they may impact women in their career choices and in their workplace functioning.

Sugar and Spice and Everything Nice

Girls with ADHD grow up under expectations to be more self-controlled, considerate, well groomed, and well behaved than boys. While "boys will be boys," we expect girls to be sweet, thoughtful, and attractive. While we teach boys to stand up for themselves, to compete, and to go after what they need, we teach girls to be more compliant, to be more concerned about the approval of others, and to compromise their own desires in order to fit in and be considerate. Many girls with ADHD grow up unable to conform to the feminine ideal. Girls that are messy, forgetful, impulsive, restless, anxious, or easily upset learn to feel badly about themselves. These problems with self-esteem only increase during adolescence and adulthood. As a result, many women with ADHD struggle not only with ADHD symptoms themselves but also with more frequent anxiety and depression compared to men with ADHD.

Greater Demands Placed on Women

Although men's roles have changed significantly over the past generation, with many men becoming more involved as parents and in maintaining the home, the greater burden for child care, meal preparation, and housekeeping continues to fall to women. While men may take jobs that require frequent travel or may stay late at the office to catch up on work during a crunch period, most women don't have these opportunities due to the demands of child care. As a result of these multiple competing demands, women with ADHD tend to live under greater stress than their male counterparts do. As I've noted frequently throughout this book, increased stress leads to increased ADHD symptoms, which become an ongoing negative loop, then lead to further stress. Many women are caught in a perpetual cycle of playing catch up or of responding to self-generated crises because they have too many balls in the air with work responsibilities, child care, meals, and housekeeping.

Many Women with ADHD Don't *Have* a Support System, They *Are* the Support System

In certain workplace situations, ADHD symptoms may have a much greater impact on women than on men because of the differences in social roles and expectations. Employment that provides private offices, interesting, challenging work, and support staff tends to be much more ADHD friendly. Historically, however, jobs such as these are more likely to be held by males. Despite all of the advances women have achieved in the workplace, most entrepreneurs and most top-level managers continue to be male, while most administrative and executive support positions continue to be held by females. Instead of having the opportunity to create a support system, many women in the workplace are required to *be* the support system for their supervisors.

> *Col. and Mrs. McAndrews were both diagnosed with ADHD following the diagnosis of their teenage son. Col. Mc.A. was an intelligent, high-ranking military officer. He was opinionated, short tempered, blunt, argumentative, impatient, and sure of himself (a good example of how a list of ADHD traits can, under certain circumstances, be a list of admired male attributes!). He was also surrounded by a squadron of lower-ranking people at his beck and call.*
>
> *With his dominating personality and intelligence, in combination with support provided by lower-ranking personnel who could compensate for his ADHD, Col. Mc.A. had risen through the ranks. His aides read and summarized reports, minimizing his ADHD difficulty with concentration while reading. Since his dictated letters were typed by his secretary, his own careless errors and misspellings were nowhere in evidence. Mrs. Mc.A. reported that her husband often had no pocket change, usually borrowed money for lunch, and frequently forgot to put gas in the car. His aides were quite used to his habits and covered for him. His energy, intelligence, and strong will got him where he was, and the structured hierarchy of the military helped compensate for his ADHD challenges.*
>
> *Mrs. Mc.A., in contrast, had no such support system. In fact, as is true of most women, she was expected to be the family support system. While Col. Mc.A. was feared and revered,*

(story continued)
Mrs. Mc.A. was seen as the family "flake." Her disorganization, forgetfulness, and emotional reactivity negatively affected everyone in the family. Whereas Col. Mc.A. was too important to be bothered with details like picking up the dry cleaning and remembering the kids' dental appointments, Mrs. Mc.A. was expected to attend to multiple detailed tasks as part of her job as wife and mother.

Thus, Col. Mc.A., in spite of his ADHD, had a successful career and was viewed as brilliant, dynamic, and forceful, whereas Mrs. Mc.A., because of her ADHD, was viewed as a generally poor housekeeper and as disorganized, unstable, and ineffective in disciplining her children.

ADHD symptoms are always viewed within a context. One context can compensate for ADHD symptoms, while another can exacerbate them. The contexts in which the McAndrewses functioned were profoundly influenced by gender expectations and biases.

How Do Women's Roles Interact with ADHD in the Workplace?

On the job, women are often expected to play a workplace version of the wife. This supportive role is currently called "administrative assistant" and was formerly called "secretary." While men at work are advised to compensate for ADHD symptoms, whenever possible, by delegating responsibilities for details and paperwork to a support person, all too often, a woman with ADHD does not have this option. In fact, she may be expected to *be* that support person.[2]

Many of the tactics recommended in Chapter 3 to improve job performance can only be applied by people who are self-employed, who have a support person, or who do much of their work independently from others. These coping skills are not typically within the realm of possibility for women who work as secretaries, office managers, teachers, nurses, dental assistants, or administrative assistants.

Multitasking—having to juggle multiple responsibilities while paying attention to detail, particularly in situations in which one is frequently interrupted—poses particular difficulty for both men and women with ADHD. However, while men in many types of positions may be able to reduce such demands, these are the very tasks that constitute the bulk of the work done by support people—who are often women.

Juggling Home and Work Responsibilities

Men often have ADHD coping tactics available to them on the home front, just as they do at work, tactics that are not available to many women for reasons that parallel male/female workplace roles. Many men with ADHD depend on a non–ADHD spouse to be social secretary, homemaker, primary parent, and family organizer and expect her to take responsibility for maintaining and managing, in ways both large and small, the household. These wives often report that their ADHD husbands are typically late, cannot be expected to remember important events in the lives of their children, and experience such overload at work that they forget to make phone calls or run errands on their way to or from work.

All of this changes, however, when it is the wife rather than the husband who has ADHD. A wife with ADHD cannot afford to let things slide at home; if Mom is a couch potato after work, the family system rapidly falls apart because meals are not prepared, soccer practice is missed, and the kids are unkempt and undisciplined.

Women are experiencing frustration and at times sheer exhaustion as they try to perform all the functions of full-time homemaker and mother while simultaneously working full time. When ADHD is an added factor, a woman's stress level can be tremendous and can have a huge impact on her workplace functioning.

Going to Work May Be Easier Than Staying Home!

In spite of the tremendous stress of being a working woman, mother, and household manager, some women with ADHD actually experience enormous relief by going to work! This is certainly not true for all jobs, but in some positions, women experience a greater ease of functioning because the distractions and interruptions are fewer and the responsibilities are more defined and limited at work than at home.

Naomi, the mother of two school-age children, worked in a professional position reviewing grant proposals, a job she found rewarding. Naomi's ADHD crisis occurred when ADHD was diagnosed in first one and then the other of her two children. Given their need for treatment, tutoring, and structure, Naomi decided it would be best to quit her job and focus her time and energy at home. Six months after that decision, she felt she was falling apart. Recognizing many of the same symptoms in herself that she saw in her children, Naomi sought an evaluation; she, too, was diagnosed with ADHD.

In her previous lifestyle, Naomi's moderate ADHD symptoms had been well managed owing to a quiet, orderly daytime routine and reasonable support with household responsibilities. In her new life as full-time homemaker, her ADHD symptoms were intensified. Suddenly, her days had little structure. Not earning any income, she now felt obliged to do all the housework and to cook all the family meals (rather than spending extra

(story continued)

money on prepared or carry-out food). She was around her children without the support of her husband many more hours during the week and discovered that the children's noise, arguments, and interruptions made her far less efficient than when both she and her husband were home together.

After understanding her ADHD symptoms and the structure and supports she needed, Naomi decided to return to her former employment. The family soon regained its equilibrium, and Naomi's self-esteem returned once she found herself back in an environment in which she could function more effectively.

Playing the Support Role at Work

Having ADHD doesn't mean you cannot effectively function in a support-staff position, but it does mean that you need to be aware of how you are affected by ADHD and that you will need to learn effective ways to compensate for your ADHD symptoms. Here are two stories of women with ADHD in administrative assistant positions. One decided to leave her position; the other learned ways to successfully compensate and became very effective in her role.

Female Administrative Assistant with ADHD: A Bad Match

Irene was employed as the administrative assistant to a highly placed boss. The boss was a woman whose judgment, people skills, and grasp of the big picture were excellent. She needed an administrator who could handle details for her, manage her

Female Administrative Assistant with ADHD: A Bad Match *(continued)*

schedule, protect her from unnecessary interruptions, and diplomatically fend off nonurgent phone calls. Irene, although smart and highly motivated, was severely affected by ADHD. She had chronic problems with timeliness, was frequently confused when trying to recall names and dates, and responded with frustration to the visitors and phone calls she was forced to deal with as the administrative assistant. In response to the frustration she felt with demands and interruptions, Irene tended to make unilateral decisions to improve the efficiency of the office. These decisions were made with good intentions but with little consideration of the effect they would have on her boss or on the other people who worked under her boss.

As tension built between her boss and her, Irene sought ADHD–related career counseling. The Myers-Briggs Type Indicator (MBTI) revealed that Irene's ADHD problems with time management, memory, and organization were not the only cause of her difficulty. The MBTI results suggested that Irene was not cut out to be in a position that required her to interact with others all day long and to be sensitive to their needs. She tended to be impatient and somewhat abrupt and was more concerned with results than with the effects of her actions on others.

Irene decided to transfer within her organization to a position that did not require her to constantly interact with the public and focus on the needs of her boss. She was much happier working on a team whose task was to publish a monthly internal newsletter. She was able to quietly focus on her task without all the interpersonal demands. Working on a team meant that any minor errors would be caught before the publication date, allowing her to focus on her writing skills.

Female Administrative Assistant with ADHD: A Good Match

Marge, a woman with ADHD, was hired for a position as an administrative assistant in a large organization. She was aware of her problems with planning and organization, which were similar to Irene's, but was able to cope with them in a more effective fashion. Although she, too, had an ADHD tendency toward poor time management, she went to extraordinary lengths to always arrive at work on time or even early. When she realized she was having organizational difficulties, she talked to her boss before the problems became catastrophic. Her boss, sensing her very real motivation, offered to send her to a series of courses on time management and organizational skills. The courses turned out to be very helpful to Marge. Most important, however, were her people skills. Marge genuinely liked interacting with people, both on the phone and in person. Her professional style and her warm manner went a long way to make up for her occasional forgetfulness and her struggles to keep up with the flow of paperwork.

Both Marge and Irene were troubled by ADHD symptoms that were incompatible with their job requirements. The differences in their situations had to do with how well their personality types matched their job descriptions. Even without ADHD, Irene would have continued to feel frustrated in her position, whereas Marge found her contact with people and her helping role very fulfilling.

Having a Support Person at Work

Although the great majority of women never reach the level of authority in an organization at which they enjoy the privilege of having a support person, a small but increasing number of women have earned advanced degrees and have risen through the ranks to the level at which they have administrative support. The key is to understand exactly what kinds of support you need and then collaborate with your support person to make sure that they can provide it to you.

Mary was an attractive, well-dressed, middle-aged woman who had gone back to school in midlife to earn a law degree. She had worked at home as a housewife and mother for many years, a job she had managed fairly well, but it had never fully satisfied her. Mary found, to her delight, that school was a "piece of cake" compared to the responsibilities of taking care of her husband, home, and children. She graduated with honors and was offered an interesting job as legal counsel for a large nonprofit organization.

Although she had done well in law school, Mary found that in her new position, with its multiple demands and unclear structure, she was having trouble staying organized and focused. To her dismay, her first performance review emphasized her difficulties with planning and organization.

When her son was diagnosed with ADHD in college, Mary recognized many of the same patterns in herself. After her initial performance review at work, she was spurred to seek her own evaluation for ADHD. Through an assessment, she learned her hunch was correct. Although medication was prescribed for her ADHD, which she found helpful, her biggest improvement at work resulted from her own detailed analysis of her job difficulties and in a reconsideration of the duties performed by her half-time administrative assistant.

In counseling, Mary was able to pinpoint the types of activities that caused her the most difficulty: keeping track of deadlines, paperwork requirements, and juggling a complicated schedule of meetings and travel. She was able to work out a new

(story continued)
distribution of tasks between herself and her half-time assistant. The scheduling and coordinating tasks were given to the assistant, leaving Mary free to do the things she did well and enabling her to stay on track.

Interpersonal Issues at Work

Interpersonal issues at work can sometimes be more difficult for women with ADHD than for their male counterparts for several reasons. A number of traits associated with ADHD—being assertive, independent, impatient, and inclined to interrupt; having a tendency to take risks—are traits that are more commonly considered masculine. When a man exhibits these traits, he may be viewed as strong or gutsy; unfortunately, these same traits are far less tolerated in women.

Women are expected to be more socially adept, persuasive, diplomatic, sensitive, and responsive. Studies have shown that girls with ADHD tend to suffer more interpersonal distress than do boys with ADHD. There is an expectation that girls will be more verbally adept from a very early age. Social IQ is expected in girls and women; when this is lacking owing to ADHD, they are less able to fulfill their social role expectations.

Women are raised to fit in, to be accepted by, and to belong to a group of peers. Interpersonal relationships, friendships, and work relationships are more essential, on average, to women than to men. As a result, women with ADHD who have limited social skills suffer more self-doubt, self-recrimination, and unhappiness than do men with the same ADHD symptoms.

Women may also often have difficulty when they are called on to set limits with others or to ask for the assistance and accommodations they need. Here again, the social conditioning that all female members of our society receive—to be pleasing to others and to place oneself last—takes an especially difficult toll on women with ADHD, whose need to be self-nurturing is even greater than that of other women.

Conclusion

To summarize, women with ADHD in the workplace face a number of challenges that differ from those of men:

- They are more likely to be hired for the very jobs that are most difficult for people with ADHD—detail-oriented support jobs.
- They must simultaneously meet the tremendous combined responsibilities of work, home, and children.
- They are placed under different and in some ways more demanding social expectations at work.
- Their ADHD traits may be seen in a more negative light than those of men are.

Given the importance of relationships and interpersonal communication, it may be even more critical for women than for men to find a work situation that is supportive, friendly, and encouraging. Women with ADHD need to become more conscious of the social and emotional demands placed on them both at home and at work and to seek jobs that are less stressful and demanding. This may mean looking for work outside the support and caretaker roles that women have traditionally filled in the past.

This chapter introduces a variety of technology supports that can reduce the negative impact of some aspects of ADHD and improve your ability to be more organized and productive at work.

16

Using Technology to Manage Workplace Challenges

Most of the challenges of ADHD in the workplace are related to what we call "executive functions." These are the skills that are required to set goals, make plans, and ultimately reach your goals. Lots of skills are involved in good executive functioning. You may feel you are good at some of these but struggle with others. In general, executive functions include the following skills:

- Planning
- Organizing
- Managing time
- Making decisions
- Prioritizing
- Getting started
- Persisting
- Sustaining focus
- Paying attention to detail
- Staying focused on your long-term goal

- Solving problems and changing plans as circumstances change
- Organizing and synthesizing your thoughts verbally or in writing

Fortunately many smartphone apps and software applications can be very useful to support executive functions and help you to build stronger executive functioning skills. These productivity tools are not specific to ADHD. They can be helpful to anyone who wants to become more focused, efficient, and productive. There are numerous tools on the market, with more being released each day. The explosion of these types of applications has been enormous, which is both a blessing and a curse. It can be difficult, with so many choices, to find the best applications to suit your needs. In this chapter, I have partnered with two others, a highly experienced ADHD workplace coach and a technology coach, to introduce you to some of the best tools we are familiar with. What we list in this chapter is only an introduction. We encourage you to search for other productivity tools online that can address particular challenges you may experience on the job.

Tools to Help Sustain Your Focus and Improve Retention While Reading

Many if not most people with ADHD report that they have difficulty maintaining focus while reading, particularly if they are reading highly detailed material that is not inherently interesting. For example, one man was employed by a company that frequently bid on federal government contracts. He described a significant struggle when reading the many detailed pages outlining government specifications. Instead, he tended to scan the documents, often missing key pieces of information that were important as he sat down to write a proposal.

Many adults report that while they are avid readers for their own enjoyment, they still have difficulty staying focused on less engaging reading material at work.

One powerful tool that can help a reader to maintain better focus is the Kurzweil 3000 (we'll come back to this tool later, focusing on how it can help you improve your writing skills). Although highly sophisticated, this program can be used by anyone from age 6 to 96. One of the core elements of the Kurzweil 3000 is a text-to-speech function that reads aloud to the user while highlighting the text being read on the computer screen. This multisensory audio/visual input greatly increases the reader's ability to remain focused. The Kurzweil can read any digitized text. If you have materials that are in print format, they can simply be scanned into the Kurzweil and then read. Additionally, the Kurzweil encourages very active reading and improved retention of the material because it allows you to highlight key information that can then be extracted to create an outline of the text; it also allows you to insert notes into the text or outline. Kurzweil 3000 is available for Mac and PC at www.kurzweiledu.com. A web version is also available, the Firefly by Kurzweil, which is built on the technology of Kurzweil 3000.

Firefly is available for iOS in the App Store. A free version syncs with Kurzweil software (web version).

Other Reading support software options (text to speech) options include Natural Reader and ReadPlease. These are two low-cost simple text-to-speech (TTS) programs that will read selected text out loud. Natural Reader can be downloaded by visiting www.naturalreaders.com/products.php. It is available for Mac and PC in both free and paid versions. ReadPlease can be downloaded by visiting http://readplease.en.softonic.com/ and is available free for PC's.

Another option, Voice Dream, can open and read aloud a wide variety of file formats, ranging from PDF files to PowerPoint presentations. It does an excellent job reading Word files, web articles, and various ebook formats, including works from Project Gutenberg and Bookshare. Voice Dream Reader (paid version) comes standard with the Acapela Heather voice. For a modest fee, you can purchase other voices (78 voices in 20 languages to choose from). You can import files directly from DropBox, Google Drive, Pocket, Instapaper, and Evernote. Voice Dream is available for iOS in the App Store. Free and paid versions are offered.

Try various free options to see which seems to be the best fit for you. Then you may want to upgrade to a paid version that provides broader support for reading and information retention.

One big advantage of using one of these software programs is that everything is digitized, so you can't lose your notes. And all provide some level of support to help you identify and highlight or pull out key information so you can quickly create digital notes you can refer to later.

If you typically have large quantities of written material to review, the search functions on some of these programs can make it easy for you to catch the critical elements of the document by simply entering keywords into the search function.

Tools for Organizing Your Thoughts to Write More Efficiently

Writing quickly, succinctly, and effectively poses great challenges for the majority of adults with ADHD. Even if your final written product is of high quality, chances are you've had to spend much more time producing the written document than many of your peers without ADHD would have.

Many factors can contribute to writing challenges. First, organization and prioritization skills are required for good writing. Both these executive function skills are difficult for many with ADHD. If you have difficulty prioritizing your tasks, you're likely to have difficulty prioritizing what to include and what to leave out of your written document.

And, just as you may struggle with organizing a project, you're likely to struggle with creating an organized structure for your document. Many adults with ADHD describe spending hours writing and rewriting the opening paragraph of a document, or writing far too much and then struggling to decide what portions to eliminate.

Templates can provide much-needed structure for work documents, whether they are brief emails or lengthy proposals or reports. Here are some websites on which you may find helpful templates to structure your writing, making your written communication much more efficient and focused.

Themuse.com offers many templates to help you think through critical emails. For example,

1. responding to a complicated email filled with lists of thoughts, ideas, and tasks.
2. when a colleague is making a project too difficult
3. when you have a workplace conflict and need to tell your boss

and many other common but difficult emails many of us need to write every day.

Businessballs.com offers writing tips as well as outlines and templates for various kinds of business letters and reports.

Proposaltemplatespro.com is a site that offers a variety of templates for various types of business proposals.

The bottom line is that a template or outline is the best place to start and can guide you to enter all the key elements into your written letter, document, or proposal. Write a rough draft from start to finish before you start polishing and getting feedback to prepare the final version of your written document.

Writing Supports

The more complex and creative your writing project, the more important it is to start by brainstorming ideas. You can do this individually or as a team if there is a group report or proposal that is being written.

Inspiration software is a visual tool that guides you to freely develop your ideas in a creative, nonlinear fashion. Inspiration is particularly helpful for visual thinkers or creative out-of-the-box thinkers that feel too constricted by a standard outline format. There is also Presentation Manager, a program that transforms your diagrams, mind maps, and outlines into a slide presentation. Inspiration is available for the Mac and PC at www.inspiration.com.

Inspiration Maps brings visual thinking to the iPad with easy transfer from the iPad to Inspiration on the computer. Inspiration Maps is available for iOS in the App Store in both free and paid versions.

Mindomo and Mindmeister are simpler mind mapping tools and are available for iOS in the App Store. They are both available in free and paid versions.

If you are someone who talks about your ideas much more easily than you can express them in writing, then you may find Dragon NaturallySpeaking (available for Mac and PC) very useful for writing first drafts. After a brief period of training the software to recognize your pronunciation, you are all set to talk to your computer and see your words appear on the screen. Dragon allows you to dictate emails, search the web, and dictate reports or any other type of document. Dragon Dictate is available for iOS in the App Store for free.

Support in Recording and Recalling What's Been Said

Many adults with ADHD experience tremendous difficulty with auditory verbal memory (recalling what's been said). Particularly when they are in a lengthy meeting, lecture, or training setting. It can be incredibly difficult to listen and never lose focus while simultaneously taking detailed notes for later reference. If protracted listening and note taking are challenging for you, then the Sonocent Audio Notetaker may be just the support you need. Its software offers a visual and interactive form of note taking—where audio, text, and images can be combined. Whether you're recording meetings, lectures, interviews, dictations, or even webinars, Audio Notetaker makes it easy to have a detailed record of all that's been said. It allows you to take screengrabs, import presentations slides or PDF documents, and annotate your recording with text and color to create the most comprehensive notes ever. Audio Notetaker is available for Windows and Mac at www.sonocent.com.

The Sonocent Audio Recorder is the companion app to Sonocent Audio Notetaker for Mac and PC. Using the app on iPhone, iPad, or iPod

Touch, you can capture high-quality recordings and annotate in real time using color markers, photos, and text notes. You can then upload it to your computer for access later for editing, revision, or further study. Sonocent Audio Recorder App is available for IOS from the App Store for free.

LiveScribe Pen is a smartpen that records everything you write and hear. When you use the LiveScribe pen on a LiveScribe notebook, you can tap anywhere on your notes to replay the audio from that moment in time. Your recorded notes and audio are wirelessly sent and can be securely stored in your Evernote account. (Evernote is an App that is purchased separately.) For more information on LiveScribe, go to www.livescribe.com/en-us/.

Managing Your Time on a Daily Basis

Time management difficulties are probably the most frequently mentioned challenge experienced by adults with ADHD. Good time management requires a set of time-related skills:

1. Accurately estimating the time required by tasks
2. Allocating time to top priorities
3. Arriving on time
4. Going to bed on time

The following are related to both time and task management and are best addressed with calendars and task-management systems:

5. Meeting deadlines
6. Scheduling all tasks as well as all meetings
7. Breaking complex tasks into doable chunks and scheduling a time to complete each one
8. Scheduling time to manage your time!

Let's take each of the first four time-management skills and explore how technology can help you support these skills.

Accurately Estimating Time Required by Tasks

Time Timer (see below) is a handy tool to help you see how accurate you are in your time estimations for tasks. It can be set at intervals of one hour or less and displays a round, bright-red clock face (or fraction of clock face for times less than one hour).

The red section of the round clock face gradually reduces with the passage of time, giving you a quick visual you can refer to easily as you go through your task. Set it on the amount of time you believe your task will take. Then see how accurate you are. Typically, those of us with ADHD tend to grossly underestimate time requirements. Using the time timer will help you learn whether to double or even triple your time estimates. Time timer gives you an auditory five-minute warning, and then another audible bell goes off when the time is up.

Staying on Task and on Time Throughout the Day

1. Time Timer allows you to custom create and save timers for the activities you do every day, like morning routines, meetings, or projects or to quickly customize a new timer whenever you need it. A digital form of Time Timer is available for iOS, Android, Mac, PC at www.timetimer.com/store/category/3/desktop-and-mobile.
2. Timeful will find you a good time to accomplish your goals.
   - Your events, to-dos, and good habits all appear on your daily calendar.
   - Smart suggestions to use your time wisely—tell Timeful the things you want to do, and advanced algorithms will make suggestions when to schedule them.

- Create habits that repeat daily, weekly, or monthly and track your progress.
- As you use Timeful, it gets to know you and builds a better schedule.

Timeful is available for iOS free from the App store. For more information, visit www.timeful.com.

3. 30/30 is a great iOS app to help you stay on task. Put your task list in with the amount of time you want to spend on each task (along with some break times). The 30/30 app gives you a countdown timer for each individual task with an alarm letting you know when it's time to move on to the next task. It's a great way to break things down into individual steps that help you move through your day while learning how to estimate time.

   30/30 is available for iOS free in the App Store.

Arriving on Time

Leave Now is an iOS App that tells you when to leave so you will be on time (or even early). Leave Now syncs with all your calendars, so it knows where you need to go and what time you need to be there. It uses GPS to calculate traffic based on your destination. So whether you are walking, driving, or taking public transportation, Leave Now will tell you when to leave to be on time. Leave Now is available for iOS free in the App Store.

Going to Bed on Time

To Bed is an iOS app that helps you get to bed on time. Based on your age and what time you want to wake up, To Bed calculates the best time for you to go to bed. Simply put in your wake-up times for the week and how far in advance you want your warning alarm before bedtime. This handy app gives you a warning notification that alerts you when it's time to go to bed. To Bed is available for iOS in the App Store.

f.lux is a free program that will gradually change your computer screen and other digital devices from the blue light usually emitted to warmer tones after the sun goes down. The user indicates her or his time zone so the program knows when to start the f.lux light warming trend. Sleep researchers have learned that the blue light emitted by digital devices blocks melatonin production in the brain, which results in difficulty falling asleep. So in addition to responding to a reminder to go to bed on time, be sure you haven't interfered with your sleep by spending your evening bathing your eyes in blue light. Visit justgetflux.com to download the app free for Mac OS X. It is also available for Windows, Linux, and iPhone/iPad.

Task Management

Many people with ADHD have great difficulty developing a clear vision of how they should allocate their time each day to make sure the key tasks are accomplished. Instead, many just dive in and start working. They stay in reactive mode—answering emails, answering the phone, or responding to whatever paper happens to be at the top of the pile on their desk.

One of the key challenges of living with ADHD is to avoid "reactive mode" and to shift into "pro-active mode"—the mode in which you prioritize and plan and then stick to your plan rather than allowing yourself to be taken off task by something that catches your eye. There are numerous task-management systems you can use in planning the use of your time and in prioritizing your tasks.

If you recall, in the time-management section, I mentioned issues that involve both time and task management.

1. Meeting deadlines
2. Scheduling all tasks as well as all meetings
3. Breaking complex tasks into doable chunks and scheduling a time to complete each one
4. And most importantly, scheduling time to manage your time

These tasks are best addressed with calendars and task-management systems such as the ones mentioned below.

Here are a couple that seem to work well:

Google Calendar is a free, fully customizable online calendar with task list that allows you to synchronize all of your information among multiple devices.

Features include:

- Create multiple color-coded calendars
- Integrates with Gmail so you can create calendar events from your email
- Allows sharing calendars with others
- View your schedule in daily, weekly, four-day, monthly, and agenda formats
- Add multiple notifications by email, pop-up, or SMS.

Google Calendar is available by signing in or creating a Google account at www.google.com/calendar.

Wunderlist is an easy-to-use task list that helps you stay on track. Wunderlist allows you to:

- Add as many lists as you need
- Share lists with others
- Sync among all devices
- Forward emails to add to your task lists

- Set due dates and add reminders by notification or email
- Add notes and checklists to tasks

Wunderlist is available on iPhone, iPad, Android, Windows Phone, Windows 8, Windows 7, Mac, Chromebook, Kindle Fire, and the Web. For more information, visit www.wunderlist.com.

Managing and Organizing Information

"I know I wrote that down somewhere. Now where is it?" If this sounds like you, then digital systems to store and organize information may be a good solution. Digital storage has a key advantage: It's always there waiting for you and can't get lost. And many systems have search functions so you can retrieve the information even if you haven't filed it in a consistent way that allows for easy retrieval.

Microsoft OneNote is one easy-to-use system that is a great way to gather and store all the information you'll need to retrieve later. You can use OneNote at home and at work to capture thoughts, ideas, and to-dos. OneNote is a computer program for freeform information gathering and multiuser collaboration. It gathers users' notes (handwritten or typed), drawings, screen clippings, and audio commentaries. Notes can be shared with other OneNote users over the Internet or a network. OneNote is available as a part of the Microsoft Office suite. It is also available as a free stand-alone application for Windows, Mac, Windows RT, Windows Phone, iOS, Android, and Symbian. A web-based version of OneNote is also available. For more information on One Note, visit www.onenote.com.

Evernote is a cloud-based platform that allows you to capture information, categorize it with tags, and store it in designated notebooks. In brief, Evernote is a place to record and save all your thoughts, notes, photos—whatever you upload—in the cloud so you can get to all of it from your computer, smartphone, tablet, or anywhere you have an Internet connection and a browser. Evernote has apps for Windows, Mac, iOS, Android, and Windows Phone. For more information, see www.evernote.com.

Corkulous idea board is an incredibly useful way to collect, organize, and share your ideas. Corkulous is a multipurpose app containing cork boards on which you can place notes, labels, photos, contacts, and tasks. Group your ideas visually on one board or spread ideas out across multiple boards (subboards also supported). Each cork board has plenty of real estate to capture your best ideas and plans. Access your ideas anywhere on your iPad, iPhone, and iPod Touch with built-in iCloud support. Share your ideas with your friends and family by storing your cork boards in DropBox. Corkulous is available for iOS in both free and paid versions. For more information, visit http://support.appigo.com/support/solutions.

Project Planning and Prioritizing

The downfall for many people with ADHD is when they are promoted to positions that require them to manage people and projects. Many more executive functioning skills are required to manage multiple people and projects. Things can quickly spiral out of control if you don't have a system to manage multiple competing tasks and responsibilities.

Priority matrix is great for managing multiple projects and responsibilities and, most important, for prioritizing your actions. You can categorize tasks by urgency or importance or come up with your own labels. You can use this app to help break down goals into smaller, measurable benchmarks as well as to organize specific projects. Priority Matrix allows you to look at just one project or all of them based on due dates. You can also integrate your calendar and import emails into the app if you purchase a paid license. Priority Matrix is available for Mac, PC, iPad, iPhone, or Android as a subscription and has a free trial; visit www.appfluence.com.

Block Distractions

The Internet is both friend and foe to people with ADHD. It offers many options for time management, task management, and information organization and storage, but at the same time, it offers a world of distractions at your fingertips.

Freedom is a program for Windows and Mac computers that helps keep you away from online distractions. You can set the program to block you from the Internet for up to eight hours at a time (if you need Internet access before your time is up, you have to reboot your computer). At the end of your time offline, Freedom allows you back on the Internet. Freedom is available for Windows and Mac. For more information, visit http://macfreedom.com.

Anti-Social is a great alternative that allows you to block distracting websites without blocking the Internet entirely. Anti-Social is available for Windows and Mac.

Medication Management

While medication management is not directly related to workplace productivity, mismanagement of your medication—forgetting to take it, running out of it—can have a big negative impact on your performance at work.

CareZone is a service that makes it easier to stay organized when managing your medication. Keep track of all your prescription and OTC medications and always have your list handy. Use the mobile app to snap a picture of your medication bottle, and the program enters all the data (including name, dosage, pharmacy, and other details). Receive a reminder when it's time to take a medication or refill a prescription. There is even a place to keep notes you can share with your doctor. CareZone also allows you to share access with your family or caregiver. CareZone is available for free on iOS, Android, and on the web. For more information, visit https://carezone.com.

The information contained in this chapter was compiled for me by Moira Williams, technology coach (www.envisiontechnology.org) and Kim Collins, adult ADHD coach (OrganizedKaos.com).

In this chapter, we look at ADHD success traits on the job by examining the success factors of ADHD author Thom Hartmann and the research conducted by Paul Gerber on highly successful adults with learning disabilities.

17

Become Your Own ADHD Success Story

ADHD success stories can be found on various ADHD websites to provide encouragement to those who are struggling with ADHD. See! You too can be successful with ADHD. Maybe you can even be successful *because of* your ADHD. Who are these success stories? There's pop star Justin Timberlake, comedian Will Smith, Olympic gold medalist Michael Phelps, Virgin Airlines founder Sir Richard Branson, socialite Paris Hilton, NFL quarterback Terry Bradshaw, and political consultant James Carville, to name a few. If you look at lists of famous successful people with ADHD, most are actors, comedians, professional athletes, high-profile businessmen, and politicians—those are professions that can lead to fame—which doesn't imply that most adults with ADHD can be found in one of these professions. You don't need to go into a high-profile, high-income career to be successful with ADHD.

There are also highly educated professionals with ADHD, such as Harvard psychiatrists Ned Hallowell and John Ratey (coauthors of the best-selling book on ADHD *Driven to Distraction*) and ADHD specialist, Steven Stanley, PhD, a former Johns Hopkins faculty member and paleobiologist, attributed much of his success to his ADHD curiosity and ability to relate obscure facts from unrelated fields to make important discoveries. ADHD is found in higher numbers among firefighters and other first responders, as well as in emergency room medical personnel, successful salespeople, people in the building trades, and all sorts of small-business owners and entrepreneurs.

It's important not just to know that there are many ADHD success stories but to understand the circumstances, choices, and traits that came together that led to their success. Many of the success stories we've cited came about "accidentally," that is, without a knowledge and awareness of the people's ADHD and an understanding of what choices would be best for them. Now that we know more about ADHD and the strengths and weaknesses associated with it, our focus should be on understanding the critical choices, patterns, and personality traits that came together and led to success. With this information, you can understand how to create a success story of your own.

What You Need to Become an ADHD Success Story

Many people ask, "What are good jobs for someone with ADHD?" Patterns have been documented. Certain professions seem to have more than their share of people with ADHD. These include:

- Sales—those with a high energy level and an extroverted personality can make the most of both in a career involving sales.
- Consulting—quite a number of business consultants have ADHD and feel that consulting is a good fit because they are working on a short-term basis with each client and enjoy the travel, stimulation, and variety of consulting.
- Business trainers—just as sales and consulting are a good fit for an extrovert with high energy and ADHD, so is the career of business trainer. It's varied and interactive and doesn't require the tedium of doing paperwork sitting at a desk.

- Building trades/construction business owners—individuals with ADHD that prefer hands-on work and have good visual/spatial ability are often drawn to the building trades—from self-employed handyman to highly skilled carpenter to business owner—these jobs allow physical movement, independence, and variety.

And the list goes on: videographer, journalist, driver/courier, photographer, artist, hospitality careers, professional chef, careers in politics, small-business owner, inventor, entrepreneur, ADHD coach, acting/show business. As you can readily see, although there are themes here—risk taking, creativity, social stimulation, movement, variety—because there is such variation among people with ADHD, there is no one-size-fits-all ADHD–friendly career.

We can learn more from the research done by Paul Gerber, a social scientist, who studied highly successful adults with learning disabilities to see what they held in common.[1] Many adults with ADHD also have learning differences, but even for those adults without learning issues, valuable information can be gleaned from Dr. Gerber's findings. He discovered common traits as well as common circumstances, which seemed to support the extraordinary success of these individuals.

The traits Gerber identified that successful adults with learning differences held in common included:

- Strong motivation
- Perseverance
- Strong desire for self-determination
- Used a planned, goal-oriented approach

In other words, these were people that would not allow challenges to get in their way. They were highly self-determined, self-directed individuals. What's more, they were able to frame their challenges in a positive light.

In addition to all these success-oriented traits, Dr. Gerber found that all of these successful adults with learning challenges knew when they needed help and were not afraid to seek it.

The good news is that the first three traits are often found in adults with ADHD.

1. **Strong motivation:** Given a subject of high interest, adults with ADHD can seem unstoppable!
2. **Determination:** Call it stubborn, call it determined, the strong-willed nature of many people with ADHD can lead to tremendous accomplishment if directed in a positive way.
3. **Strong need to control one's life and future:** Described negatively, this might be expressed as accepting supervision poorly! The adult with ADHD needs to translate his or her not liking to be told what to do into charting his or her own course.

Considered together, this trio of determination, motivation, and independence have played major roles in the success stories of adults with ADHD.

4. **Capacity to see ADHD in a positive light:** It's essential to turn the corner, no longer seeing ADHD as a disabling condition but rather looking at how some ADHD traits can be used to advantage. This positive attitude will take more work for those who have received more criticism than support in their lives. Often, counseling can help you change your self-concept from "defective" to "different"—with a recognition of all the positive traits included in that difference.
5. **A planned, goal-oriented approach:** The ability to maintain a planned, goal-oriented approach is the internal factor that requires the most work and effort for adults with ADHD to develop. Why? The problem for adults with ADHD often comes when it is time to harness all their energy, determination, and independence by charting a course and sticking to it. They must learn to be actors rather than reactors.

Ned Hallowell writes in *Answers to Distraction*[2] that many ADHD adults resist structure, feeling it will hamper their creativity and enjoyment. Dr. Hallowell explains, however, that the right kind of structure actually enhances and promotes creativity. He emphasizes how important it is for ADHD adults to be in charge of the structure rather than feel it is imposed on them (remember the need ADHD adults have to be in charge of their own destiny!).

6. **Ability to seek help when needed without becoming dependent:** Seeking help may be difficult for some adults with ADHD. Frank Sinatra's "My Way" could be their theme song. Although independence can be a very positive trait, it can become bullheadedness if taken too far. An "I don't take advice from anyone" attitude can lead to enormous problems. If you experience great discomfort when being supervised by others or when seeking advice from others, it may be extremely important for you to work on this issue in psychotherapy; you should also take extra care to work under a compatible supervisor.

External Success Factors—Finding the Right Environment to Support Success

Now let's take a look at the external factors Paul Gerber found, factors that supported the success of the adults with learning disabilities. These people found success either through sheer good fortune or through personal insight and initiative. By reading this book, you yourself have the tremendous advantage of learning from the experience of others. What did all these people have in common in their work environment?

A Mentor

Mentorship can take different forms. Mentors enjoy the role of passing on the wisdom and experience they have gained over many years in their field, and younger employees flourish under the supportive tutelage of their mentors and provide increasingly valuable support to their mentors as they grow professionally.

It can be a long-standing relationship or a series of mentors as a younger worker moves from one rung of the career ladder to the next. One highly successful young woman reported that the most important trait she sought in a supervisor was the ability to be a mentor. She actively sought supervisors whose experience was greater and whose knowledge would help her advance in her career.

Some adults with ADHD actively avoid placing themselves in the position of having mentors. Unlike the self-directed, determined young woman who readily recognized the value of a mentor, they fear that they are giving up autonomy by seeking advice. It's important to keep in mind that the guidance of a mentor is not something imposed on you; rather, it comes from a relationship you initiate and from which you directly benefit.

Positive, Supportive Coworkers

When he interviewed successful people with learning disabilities, Paul Gerber found that they worked in a friendly, supportive environment. Such an environment is just as important for people with ADHD (more about this in Chapter 9). As is true of the best academic environment, the best workplace is one in which you feel supported and encouraged. Surrounded by emotional support, you are more relaxed, less likely to make ADHD–related errors, and more able to take risks in order to grow professionally.

The power of a positive work environment is strongly reflected in Amy's story.

Amy had been diagnosed with ADHD and learning disabilities as a child. Despite a high IQ, she had never done well in school, partly because she resisted all forms of treatment and intervention.

After graduating from high school. Amy drifted from one dead-end job to another until she was hired, entirely by chance, by a couple who ran a small family business. The personal

(story continued)
chemistry between Amy and her employers was very positive. They recognized her intelligence, and she thrived in the first environment in which she felt truly appreciated. Amy became a model employee—highly reliable and enthusiastic. As she learned more and more about the business, she began to believe, for the first time, that she was smart, something her parents and teachers had always told her.

Even better, Amy's confidence helped her grow in other ways. She became friendly with the owner's son, a college student her own age. Hanging around college students for the first time in her life, she began to think of greater possibilities in her future. To her own amazement, a few years after her disastrous high school experience, she was thinking of taking college courses and realized that her future held a wide range of choices.

Amy's history is a clear example of the importance of finding positive, supportive people to work among. The couple for whom she worked served as mentors (and even quasi-parents) for her as she struggled to develop the self-esteem that had been so eroded during her school years. In the past, Amy had painfully learned that failure leads to failure; she was now in the process of learning that success breeds success!

New Work Experiences to Enhance Skills

Paul Gerber's study found that successful learning-disabled adults found work experiences that allowed them to grow and develop. For adults with ADHD, however, this aspect of a job is critical. In order to overcome difficulties with concentration, follow-through, and motivation, it is essential that individuals with ADHD find work that continues to interest them, work that allows variety and at least a moderate degree of challenge. Boredom and repetition are the dreaded components of any job for an adult with ADHD.

John had experienced success in his work life despite ADHD, which was only identified in his late fifties when his son, age twenty-five, was diagnosed. Financial success had never been a primary goal for John. Rather, he valued freedom, variety, creativity, and change. His resumé was remarkably varied. At the time of his diagnosis he was living on a sailboat with his second wife and working as a building contractor.

I met John when he was doing remodeling work for me. A voluble man, he once explained to me that whenever he became truly bored with his current job, he began making mistakes.

John was working in my kitchen, constructing a table, at the time of this particular conversation. A few minutes later, I heard a loud curse. I quickly returned to the kitchen and found him, electric saw in hand, gazing with consternation at a gash he had cut in the nearly finished tabletop. He turned to me and said, "This is one of those moments that tells me it's time to move on!" And, indeed, he did just that. When I heard from him a few months later, he had quit the home remodeling business and had started a new business with his wife.

The small line of wood putty, barely discernible on the kitchen table, has always reminded me that boredom and repetition lead to problems for many adults with ADHD. Whether you move on to an entirely new venture or find new and interesting activities within your current field, it is essential for people with ADHD to have new work experiences to grow, develop, and maintain interest.

A Work Environment in Which Help Is Available When Needed

Readily available help is, of course, a critical part of any supportive work environment and an essential feature of an ADHD–friendly workplace. I would add a qualification: that the help be available informally and on an as-needed basis. Because ADHD adults so typically have difficulty with time management, planning, and organization, it is much more helpful for them to work in an environment in which they can get an on-the-spot answer to a question than in one in which the supervisor says, "Write down your questions, and we'll talk about them in our supervisory session at the end of the week." People with ADHD, whether in an academic or a work environment, typically find that when help is provided in a procedural, bureaucratic fashion, it has limited effectiveness and is used infrequently.

A Good Fit between Skills and Job Requirements

Because people with learning disabilities and ADHD typically have strengths and weaknesses in both natural abilities and job skills, it is particularly important that the primary demands of their jobs be those that are related to their strengths and that tasks related to their natural strengths as well as skills that they have developed and that tasks related to their areas of weakness constitute a minor part of their jobs. While this combination would be beneficial to anyone, it is much more critical for those with ADHD because the difference between their skills and weaknesses is great. As many with ADHD have painfully learned, you can feel and appear incompetent if you are placed in a work (or academic) situation that calls on you to function in your areas of greatest weakness. If you are interested in developing a better understanding of your natural abilities, you might want to consider taking the Highlands Ability Test,[3] a multifaceted abilities test that can be taken online and interpreted by a professional that is certified by Highlands.

The Essential ADHD Success Factor

To the five aforementioned external factors important to job success, I would add a critical sixth element for adults with ADHD: a good fit between one's **interests** and the requirements of one's job.

The importance of interest cannot be emphasized enough! Adults with ADHD who have a high degree of interest in their work generally find that their ADHD problems (such as careless errors, forgetfulness, distractibility, poor follow-through) are minimized, while their ADHD positive traits (ability to hyperfocus for long periods of time, high energy level, determination) are stimulated. The Strong Vocational Interest Test[4] is one of the best-known measures of interest. It compares your responses to the interests of individuals that have been successful in a wide variety of fields.

Hartmann's Success Factors

Thom Hartmann, in his book *ADHD Secrets of Success*[4] talks about three other success traits he has found among successful ADHD entrepreneurs:

Individualism

Creativity

Need for high stimulation

Their individualism led them to seek entrepreneurial activities rather than remain within a bureaucratic structure. Their creativity led them to new ideas, including the envisioning of new market niches. Finally, their need for high stimulation led them to move on to new tasks, challenges, and ventures. Hartmann emphasizes that failure for such talented ADHD individuals tended to occur when they had to shift from their high-energy-high-creativity mode to a more predictable and mundane managerial mode as their enterprise developed and matured. To accommodate to this almost inevitable cycle, Hartmann suggests that such ADHD adults plan in advance to turn over management of their enterprise to others so they can move on to do what they love best—engage in the next creative adventure!

Conclusion

Researchers have spent most of their time emphasizing the negative aspects of the disorder we call ADHD. On the other hand, Paul Gerber's research stresses that it is quite possible to attain professional success despite learning disabilities (which are in many ways parallel to ADHD). Thom Hartmann goes even further: He challenges the notion that ADHD is a disorder at all. He turns the negative point of view on its head and looks at the potential good that can result from the supposedly negative symptoms of ADHD. Both authors present a hopeful message. By studying the traits shared by successful people with ADHD, you can learn ways to both take charge of your ADHD–related problems and take advantage of the positive aspects of ADHD.

Notes

1 Gerber, P., Ginzberg, R., & Reiff, H. (1992). Identifying alterable patterns in employment success for highly successful adults with learning disabilities. *Journal of Learning Disabilities, 25,* 475–487.
2 Hallowell, E., & Ratey, J. (1995). *Answers to Distraction.* New York: Pantheon.
3 Highlands Ability Battery, published by the Highlands Company, www.highlandsco.com.
4 Strong Interest Inventory, published by CPP, Inc., Sunnyvale, CA, www.cpp.com.

This final chapter summarizes the information provided in this book and offers a framework for you to build on in creating your own ADHD workplace success story.

18

Putting It All Together to Achieve Your Career Goals

Make the Career Process ADHD Friendly

This book has covered a broad range of material concerning attention deficit hyperactivity disorder in the workplace. At this point you may feel a little overwhelmed, not knowing where or how to begin. You may harbor a secret wish that someone would just identify the perfect job for you so you could go find it and live happily ever after, without bothering with all the issues I have discussed in this book. An understandable wish!

Of course you feel overwhelmed! This final chapter offers you something that can help you get started and that you can also use as a model for handling complicated, long-term projects: a short summary of the highlights covered in the book.

Take Charge of Your ADHD So It Won't Take Charge of You!

Taking charge means becoming an actor rather than a reactor. What is an actor? An actor is someone who sets a course for him- or herself rather than staying in a reactive mode. Many people with ADHD have lived their entire lives in a reactive mode, responding to whatever random opportunity or event comes their way. The most important message of this book is that to take charge of your ADHD, of your career, and of your life, you need to develop the attitude and skills of an actor.

Actors act on their world; reactors react to their world.

An actor is a problem solver, a solution seeker. ADHD actors work to control events inside themselves by managing their ADHD symptoms and outside themselves by finding or creating an ADHD–friendly environment. These actors seek ways to work with and to even profit from their ADHD rather than allow their ADHD to work against them.

Taking charge means managing troublesome ADHD patterns. You can't tackle them all at once, and you shouldn't try to tackle them all alone. With the help of a counselor or coach, you can pinpoint your most troublesome ADHD patterns, identify which one to work on first, and then problem solve to find the best management techniques. After you have found the best approaches, don't expect yourself to change overnight. Building new habits takes practice.

Remember the four Ps

- Pinpoint
- Prioritize
- Problem solve
- Practice

Don't Approach Habits Like a Crash Diet! They Take Time to Develop

Many adults with ADHD report that they never really learned how to develop habits as a child. Many adults with ADHD treat habit development like a crash diet. They make a resolution, expect perfection of themselves, and quit in defeat a few days or weeks later. A habit takes lots of repetition to develop. Parents have to remind their children hundreds of times to brush their teeth before the children develop the habit. Just as you shouldn't expect a child to develop a new habit overnight, neither should you expect this of yourself. Learning ADHD management skills is the process of developing many small habits. Don't despair. Start small, and keep at it (a coach or counselor can help).

Taking Charge Means Understanding Yourself

For real understanding, testing is helpful. Not everyone needs every type of test. At a minimum, you should complete the ADHD Workplace Questionnaire in this book and take the Myers-Briggs Type

Indicator.[1] Both are quick and usually inexpensive. Learning disability testing should only be considered if you answered "yes" to a number of items in the section "Related Cognitive Difficulties" in the ADHD Workplace Questionnaire. Interest and ability testing can be useful if you don't feel you have a good idea of yourself in these areas. The better you understand yourself, your values, your personality, your talents, your weak points, and your interests, the better the career choice you will make.

Create an ADHD–Friendly Environment

Taking charge means finding or creating an ADHD–friendly environment. One of the most damaging effects of ADHD is the relentless stream of negative feedback received over a lifetime. As an adult, you have the chance to look for employers who will enjoy and appreciate your best traits. Look for workplace environments that are not rigid, rule bound, and focused on details. This doesn't mean you don't want to change some of your ADHD patterns. But having coworkers and supervisors who are impatient, irritated, and frequently critical of your behavior is not likely to help you make positive changes. By contrast, feeling good about yourself and your accomplishments at work can give you the strength and motivation to work on problem areas more effectively.

Finding people who like and appreciate you is wonderful, but you also need to work toward creating an environment that is truly ADHD friendly. Reading Chapter 1, "An ADHD–Friendly Work Environment," will help you recognize some of the factors to look for.

Put yourself where you'll be appreciated!

Advocate for Yourself at Work

Taking charge means advocating for yourself at work. Set a goal to become an expert on yourself in the workplace. While your employer can provide some accommodations, the responsibility for career success lies with you. Here are some guidelines to follow as you advocate for yourself:

1. Show that you are motivated to succeed on the job.
2. Approach problems with a positive attitude.
3. Be specific in describing your needs to your employer.
4. Make reasonable requests.
5. Don't approach the issue of accommodations from an adversarial position but rather from a win–win position.
6. Don't just focus on what you need or want; demonstrate to your supervisor that you are working hard to overcome problem patterns.

Taking charge means understanding your legal rights.

- Carefully consider the pros and cons of disclosing your ADHD.
- Carefully consider the pros and cons of taking legal steps to defend your rights at work.
- Consult an attorney when all other efforts have failed to produce workable results.
- Understand your responsibilities and the responsibilities of your employer under the Americans with Disabilities Act.[2]

Make ADHD–Smart Career Choices

Taking charge means making ADHD–smart career choices or changes. With the assistance of an ADHD expert, learn as much as possible about your strengths, weaknesses, interests, special talents, and

ADHD needs. Then carefully consider all your options. Ask yourself the following questions:

- Can I make changes in me that will improve my current job?
- Can I make changes in my job that will improve my performance?
- Do I have the right career but the wrong job?
- Do I need to rethink my career?

Conclusion

You can create your own ADHD success story by taking charge of your ADHD.

Work toward developing a positive, proactive stance toward your work life:

1. Realistically assess your ADHD traits and learn how to manage them.
2. Understand your interests, abilities, and personality traits.
3. Recognize and use the positive side of your ADHD.
4. Actively develop ADHD success traits.
5. Actively seek an ADHD–friendly work environment.
6. Become an effective self-advocate at work.
7. Remember the positive ADHD traits found in successful adults.
8. Appreciate the positive side of your ADHD and put it to work for you.

Taking charge means approaching ADHD with a positive attitude.

Making the career choices and changes you want will take time and perseverance. You don't need to do it all on your own, and you shouldn't try to do it all at once. By putting into action the steps outlined in this book, you can become your own ADHD success story!

Notes

1 Myers, I. B., & Briggs, K. C. (1976). *Myers-Briggs Type Indicator*. Palo Alto, CA: Consulting Psychologists Press.
2 Americans With Disabilities Act, U.S. Code, vol. 42, secs. 12101 et seq (1990).

Appendix

ADHD Workplace Questionnaire

The ADHD Workplace Questionnaire has been developed to help you think about the effects of your ADHD at work in a systematic fashion. This questionnaire can be used by your therapist or counselor to help you consider issues of workplace functioning. It may be helpful to use this questionnaire with a career counselor if you are in the process of career change.

This questionnaire is not a diagnostic tool. It is meant to be used by adults who have already been diagnosed with ADHD as a means of pinpointing ADHD–related challenges in the workplace as a first step toward problem solving. To be most effective, it should be filled out by both you and someone at work who knows you and your work habits well. If you are not comfortable having someone at work complete the questionnaire, it may be helpful to have a spouse, a good friend, or your therapist go over the items with you. Why? Because many adults with ADHD are not accurate self-observers. You may be doing things you are unaware of, or you may be doing them to a much greater extent than you realize. As part of the process of self-analysis, which is essential to solving your workplace problems, you need an accurate assessment. Honest feedback, given supportively by someone you trust, can be a valuable piece of this assessment process.

The questionnaire is divided into several sections. In the first section, the questions focus on how ADHD traits may affect your capacity to perform your work. In the second section, the focus is on how your ADHD traits may affect interpersonal relationships at work. The third section focuses on cognitive issues related to ADHD, and the final section focuses on issues in the physical environment of the workplace.

ADHD Workplace Questionnaire

Terms such as "frequently" or "very" or "prone to" are open to interpretation. Don't overfocus on any one answer. You are searching for patterns and tendencies. All individuals encounter some of the problems listed from time to time. This questionnaire is meant to help you pinpoint areas of difficulty at work so you can begin to problem solve.

Please rate yourself using the following code:

0—Not at all
1—Slightly
2—Moderately
3—Considerably
4—Extremely

Issues to which you assign a score of 3 or 4 are clearly areas of concern. Generally, it is more helpful to look at the score for a cluster of questions than for single scattered questions. Therefore, average your responses in each cluster of questions. If the average is 3 or 4 for any cluster, this may be an area for which you need to actively seek solutions.

ADHD Patterns Affecting Work Performance

Inattention/Distractibility

1. ____ I frequently shift from one activity to another at work.
2. ____ I am easily distracted by the conversations of coworkers.
3. ____ My mind wanders when I try to read reports and memos.
4. ____ It is hard for me to return to a task after an interruption.
5. ____ My best work is done early or late in the workday, when there are few distractions.
6. ____ It is difficult for me to listen consistently during long meetings.

7. ____ I am prone to leave tasks incomplete because I jump to something else.
8. ____ It is hard to stay focused on one thing because other ideas intrude.
9. ____ I daydream frequently at work.

Hyperfocusing

1. ____ I become so involved in one project that I forget about other responsibilities.
2. ____ When I am really interested in a project, I lose all track of time and can work nonstop for hours.
3. ____ Sometimes I am oblivious to things occurring around me because I'm so wrapped up in what I'm doing.

Impulsivity

1. ____ I tend to jump into projects with little planning.
2. ____ I enthusiastically begin projects, but soon lose interest.
3. ____ I am prone to do things on the spur of the moment, according to my mood.
4. ____ I typically agree or offer to do something without considering other commitments.

Hyperactivity/Restlessness

1. ____ I feel very restless during meetings.
2. ____ I tend to doodle or fiddle with small objects during meetings.
3. ____ It's hard for me to stay at my desk for long stretches of time.
4. ____ I seem to take more breaks than my coworkers because I need to move around.

5. ____ I tend to tap, fidget, swing my leg, and so on when sitting.
6. ____ I prefer work that allows me to move from one job site to another.
7. ____ I seem to move at a faster pace than the rest of the world.

Need for Stimulation/Intolerance of Routine

1. ____ I become bored very easily.
2. ____ I have quit a job simply because I needed something new.
3. ____ I am much happier thinking up new ideas than carrying them out.
4. ____ I am a "big picture" person who dislikes tending to the details.
5. ____ When doing detailed work, I am prone to make careless errors.

Memory

1. ____ I tend to forget things I have been told.
2. ____ If I don't write down information, I'm likely to forget it.
3. ____ I am prone to forget to do what I have promised.
4. ____ I frequently misplace personal items.
5. ____ It's hard for me to remember to do a task at a particular time.

Time Management

1. ____ I am frequently late for work.
2. ____ I am often late for meetings during the day.

3. ____ I usually underestimate how much time a task will require.
4. ____ I try to do too many things at once.
5. ____ I tend to procrastinate.
6. ____ It's hard for me to meet deadlines.

Paperwork

1. ____ My desk at work is usually overflowing.
2. ____ I am often behind on my paperwork.
3. ____ I tend to make careless errors when doing paperwork.
4. ____ I tend to read things too quickly and to miss important information.
5. ____ My filing system is disorganized.
6. ____ I am usually behind on my filing.
7. ____ I have difficulty keeping accurate records of expenses and activities.

Organization

1. ____ I like structure but have difficulty creating it.
2. ____ When I try to organize, I'm back to the same old clutter within a few days.
3. ____ I have difficulty in consistently using a calendar to schedule my day.
3. ____ Long-term projects are hard for me to organize.
4. ____ I often go through my day without a plan, simply reacting to events.
5. ____ I tend to improvise rather than plan in advance.

Interpersonal Stresses Related to ADHD Patterns

Many of the patterns already listed affect interpersonal interactions at work. However, the emphasis in the first section of the questionnaire has been on job performance. In this second section, we shift the focus to help you examine how your ADHD patterns may affect your ability to get along with and work well with others.

Distractibility

1. ____ I have trouble listening consistently when someone is speaking to me.
2. ____ I tune out in meetings and may seem uninterested.
3. ____ I tend to avoid interactions with others in order to focus on my work.

Hyperfocusing

1. ____ When I'm wrapped up in my work, I sometimes don't hear others when they speak to me.
2. ____ Sometimes I'm so involved in my own thoughts that I don't stop to greet or interact with coworkers as I pass them.
3. ____ I am prone to ignore the importance of communicating with others about the work I am doing.

Impulsivity

1. ____ I tend to interrupt others in conversation.
2. ____ Sometimes I say things before thinking of possible consequences.
3. ____ I tend to do things as they occur to me without stopping to consult with my supervisor or coworkers.

4. ____ I may be considered a "loose cannon" at times because of my tendency to react impulsively and unpredictably.

Hyperactivity/Restlessness

1. ____ I may make others uncomfortable by fidgeting or fiddling while listening to them.
2. ____ I become obviously frustrated with the slower pace of others.
3. ____ I am impatient with the lengthy discussions that take place before any decision is made.
4. ____ I dislike just sitting around talking at meetings, giving others the impression their company is not important to me.

Need for Stimulation/Intolerance of Routine

1. ____ I may irritate others by leaving the details of a job to them.
2. ____ I may appear irresponsible because I like to think up new ideas but rely on others for the follow-through.
3. ____ I am prone to avoid the routine, boring tasks, which sometimes places a burden on others.

Memory

1. ____ I make promises and then forget to keep them.
2. ____ I often forget things people have told me.
3. ____ I tend to rely on others to remind me of things.
4. ____ I frequently need to borrow items from others because I have forgotten or misplaced my own.

Time Management

1. ____ I am frequently late for work.
2. ____ I am often late for meetings during the day.
3. ____ I tend to keep people waiting because I am running late.
4. ____ It's hard for me to meet deadlines others give me.

Paperwork

1. ____ If someone needs a document from me, I typically have difficulty finding it right away.
2. ____ I rarely turn in paperwork on time, sometimes making it necessary for others to remind me.
3. ____ I tend to skim through memos and letters others write to me, often missing important details contained in them.

Organization

1. ____ My disorganization interferes with the productivity of coworkers.
2. ____ I have difficulty managing and supervising others.
3. ____ I tend to rely on others to provide structure on long-term projects.

Autonomy Issues

1. ____ I dislike being closely supervised.
2. ____ I have been described as argumentative.
3. ____ I have been described as stubborn.
4. ____ I tend to talk on and on about something if I think I'm right.
5. ____ I am happier working independently than on a team.

Emotional Reactivity

1. ____ I tend to react defensively when criticized.
2. ____ I have low tolerance for frustration.
3. ____ I tend to have strong emotional reactions.
4. ____ I have lost my temper at work.
5. ____ I easily become impatient with others.

Emotional Sensitivity

1. ____ My feelings are easily hurt at work.
2. ____ I find it hard to work when there are interpersonal conflicts, even if they don't directly involve me.
3. ____ Having a positive relationship with my supervisor is very important to me.
4. ____ It is hard for me to accept constructive criticism.

Emotional Insensitivity

1. ____ I am not as tuned in to the feelings of others as I should be.
2. ____ I am prone to make suggestions or comments in a non-diplomatic fashion.
3. ____ I am sometimes unaware that my behavior is upsetting to others.

Related Cognitive Difficulties

The statements in the following list do not refer to official ADHD traits but to cognitive difficulties that are often experienced by people with ADHD. Answering "yes" to some of these questions may indicate that a learning disability evaluation is in order.

Related Cognitive Problems

1. ____ Sometimes I become so mentally exhausted that I can hardly think.
2. ____ I seem to take longer than others to learn new material.
3. ____ I have always had problems with spelling.
4. ____ I know what I want to say, but it's hard to put my thoughts in writing.
5. ____ It is much easier for me to learn from written than from verbal presentations.
6. ____ Reading has always been laborious for me; I would much rather learn by being shown or told than by reading.
7. ____ I have difficulty reading maps or following directions to unfamiliar locations.
8. ____ Math has always been difficult for me.

Environmental Sensitivities Related to ADHD

The following sensitivities are not recognized as ADHD symptoms but are often reported by individuals with ADHD and need to be recognized and managed.

Sensitivity to the Physical Work Environment

1. ____ Fluorescent lights bother me.
2. ____ I am very sensitive to noises in the workplace.
3. ____ I am very sensitive to the air temperature at work.
4. ____ It is hard for me to work in a room that has no natural light.

5. ____ Unpleasant physical surroundings greatly detract from my ability to work effectively.
6. ____ I am very sensitive to crowded work spaces.

How to Use the ADHD Workplace Questionnaire

The preceding questionnaire is not a test or diagnostic tool but a structured questionnaire designed to assist you in examining the difficulties you, as an adult with ADHD, may experience in the workplace. Several chapters in this book are devoted to practical suggestions for managing difficulties in each of these areas.

The most effective way to use the information from the questionnaire is by following these steps:

1. Identify your problem clusters—those clusters of questions in which you assigned yourself many 3s and 4s.
2. Rank these clusters in order, starting with the cluster you feel has the most negative impact on your work performance.
3. Do not try to tackle everything at once.
4. Pick a cluster to work on and engage in creative problem solving with yourself, your counselor, and, if appropriate, your supervisor at work. Solutions may involve a number of things, including (1) changing habits on your part, (2) environmental changes, such as a more organized or less distracting work space, and (3) alterations in work patterns or job description to better suit your needs.

Index